Contents

	Foreword	6
	Preface	7
	Acknowledgements	9
1.	Introduction	10
2.	Invention, Innovation and Small Business	17
3.	Research and Development and the Small Firm	27
4.	Technology Diffusion	44
5.	Clusters and Knowledge Flows	59
6.	Higher Education Spin-offs	71
7.	Global Start-ups and business development	89
8.	Innovation Performance Indicators	106

9. Conclusions

Foreword

With a modern society that is seeing fast changing social, economic, political and cultural developments never before has innovation been more important for small businesses. As a consequence the study of innovation is a fast developing area with publication of a number of leading texts. These however tend to investigate innovation management activities in large businesses with limited consideration of the small business area. This is disproportional to the amount of research activity that is being undertaken in the small business field. These seminal texts into innovation management in large organizations have previously considered popular, as well as requisite, concepts such as disruptive technology and more recently open innovation and the "fuzzy front end". Moreover, innovation is seen in terms of creativity and the generation of new ideas. It is evident that whereas large companies are good at implementing innovation, small companies are better at generating new ideas although research tells us that only around 10% will be commercially viable. Contributing to this innovation activity there will also be different forms of innovation including product, process and service innovations and also radical and incremental innovations.

In response to this gap this volume considers innovation and small business with particular reference to the innovation process. Here an approach appropriate to small businesses is taken by considering the distinction between invention and innovation as well as research and development in the context of the small firms. In addition, technology diffusion, clusters and knowledge flows, higher education spin-offs, global start-ups and innovation performance indicators are also considered with particular reference to the small business sector.

Preface

In modern technological society small businesses are expected to have an innovative role in the emerging knowledge economy, especially at an international level (EC, 2005; BERR, 2008). In fact the effective use of technological innovation is considered to be a prerequisite for small business survival (Packham, 2002; Packham et al, 2005). It has long been recognised that the small business sector is important for economic growth and it has been noted that there is a need for an international focus on small businesses having access to international markets (OECD, 2005). Within this context it has been acknowledged that small business development programmes and assistance should enable them to take advantage of innovative global technologies (OECD, 2005). Although significant opportunities are presented to small businesses through the adoption of new technologies there needs to be awareness to the barriers of implementation and this has led researchers to focus on adoption factors (Parasuraman, 2000). Indeed, there has been little success linking the determinants of adoption in small businesses with expected outcomes such as innovation, apart from specialised research and development (R&D) intense sectors (Thomas and Simmons, 2010).

Small businesses with an above average absorptive capacity tend to exhibit experience, knowledge, a skills base, knowledge creation and sharing processes (Cohen and Levinthal, 1990; Zahra and George, 2002; Gray, 2006). Their effective use of networking and an optimal use of technological innovation are the focus of this first volume. It is therefore hoped that this volume will provide a greater understanding of these innovation processes for small businesses.

References

Cohen, W. and Levinthal, D. (1990) Absorptive Capacity: A New Perspective on Learning and Innovation, *Administrative Science Quarterly*, 35(1), 128-152.

Department for Business, Enterprise and Regulatory Reform (BERR) (2008) *Business Plan 2008–2011*, June, London.

European Commission (EC) (2005) Implementing the Community Lisbon Programme – Modern SME Policy for Growth and Employment (COM) (2005), 551 final, November, Brussels.

Gray C. (2006) Absorptive capacity, knowledge management and innovation in entrepreneurial small firms, *International Journal of Entrepreneurial Behaviour & Research*, 12(6), 345-360.

OECD. (2005) *Small to Medium-Sized Business (SME) and Entrepreneurship Outlook*, OECD, Paris.
Packham, G., Brooksbank, D., Miller, C. and Thomas, B. (2005) Climbing the Mountain: Management Practice Adoption in Growth Oriented Firms in Wales, *Small Business and Enterprise Development*, 12, 482-497.

Packham, G. (2002) Competitive Advantage and Growth: The Challenge For Small Firms, *International Journal of Management and Decision-Making*, 3, 165-179.

1. Introduction

"Innovation is the central issue in economic prosperity"

MICHAEL PORTER (1947-)

This chapter at a glance

- Innovation and Small Business
- Small Business Innovation Networks
- Organisation of the Book

Innovation and Small Business

Small businesses are making an important contribution to the development of technological innovation within industries at regional and national levels. In fact, the European Commission (EC, 1993, 1994, 2007) has reported that this sector probably holds the key to the future renewal and growth of Europe. According to the EC small businesses are enterprises employing fewer than fifty people, with an annual turnover/balance sheet total not exceeding ten million euro (EC, 2005). Innovation can be defined as either the 'application of a new method or device' (Collins, 1997) or the 'successful exploitation' of a new idea (Thomas and Rhisiart, 2000). According to Baregheh et al. (2009) innovation is 'the multi-stage process whereby organisations transform ideas into new/improved products, services or processes, in order to advance, compete and differentiate themselves successfully in their marketplace'.

Whereas the advantages of small businesses in innovation are largely associated with flexibility, dynamism and responsiveness (Rothwell, 1994), the disadvantages are often related to a lack of financial and technological resources. This can lead to problems in their capability to absorb and diffuse technology within industrial sectors. This is a major problem in the development of the small business sector in many UK regions, especially as external inputs are of greater importance for the small firm than for the large firm during the innovation process (Allen et al., 1983). With the different levels of regional industrial development within Europe there will also be variations in the importance of innovation support to the small business (Saxenian, 1991). This inequality can make access to knowledge, technology and human resources more difficult, and will affect not only the development of small businesses within regions, but also the efficiency and effectiveness of the regional innovation system. Regional policy needs to respond to these variations, and develop innovation support networks that are sensitive to the needs of small business.

Uyarra (2005) has investigated theoretical issues and empirical evidence of regional innovation strategies with regard to knowledge, diversity and regional innovation policies. The development of concepts concerning regional innovation has led to the new regionalist literature (Lovering, 1999) and to models of territorial innovation (Moulaert and Sekia, 1999). Such concepts include regional innovation systems, the triple helix, innovative milieu, technological districts and learning regions (Uyarra, 2005). Here there are concerns on the use of concepts including regional innovation systems to study declining economies, rural areas and peripheral regions (Doloreux, 2002; Asheim and Isaksen, 2002). It is concluded that it is rare to identify the requisite aspects for a regional system of innovation (Evangelista et al, 2002). In terms of increasing globalisation it appears sensible for small businesses to use support for their own innovation goals (Cooke, 2001) whether or not the support comes from outside or within a region (Uyarra, 2005).

Small Business Innovation Networks

It has been shown that networking is a time-consuming and demanding activity with opportunity costs for small businesses with limited resources (Rothwell, 1994). Accordingly, there is a need to enable small businesses to overcome innovation-related disadvantages associated with networking. Since this has become a key feature of industrial innovation this increases the small businesses innovatory capabilities. Negative and positive aspects of networks need to be noted since, for example, ICT systems carry dangers as well as opportunities for small businesses, especially where industry-wide operating standards lock them into large networks.

In innovation support networks technology equates with knowledge. Within university-industry link systems a multiplicity of technology transfer mechanisms are apparent, which appear to be well integrated (Cheese, 1993). Chambers of commerce who deliver innovative support to small businesses complement the higher education system. Small businesses need to co-operate through network groups to share learning and training resources and good practice. It is clear that chambers of commerce can provide support by acting as the prime entry point into the local innovation support network, by offering basic consultancy and using knowledge of the network to direct businesses, as necessary, to the agent, such as an independent research centre or a higher education institution (Cheese, 1993). A non-trivial source of the exchange of information on problems of common interest are personal contacts within an informal network (Desforges, 1985). A problem that is particularly acute for small businesses is co-operation since they tend not to be well integrated into academic/government/company networks.

A network of co-operation partners will operate to form a 'focal point' of business innovation (Martinussen, 1992). The hub of the process needs good organisation and a network of co-operation partners involving business innovation centres, technology transfer companies, science parks, and venture capital companies. These will be responsible for developing technology from a business idea to establishment of a new firm.

Organisation of the Book

This volume contains chapters concerning the innovation process and small business and considers invention, innovation and small business, research and development and the small firm, technology diffusion, clusters and knowledge flows, higher education spin-offs, global start-ups and business development and innovation performance indicators.

Chapter 2: Invention, Innovation and Small Business
This opening chapter introduces the distinction between invention and innovation and the interrelationships between invention, innovation and small business. The chapter investigates inventive activity in the modern technological setting of the 21st Century and reports on the barriers, motivations and drivers to inventors becoming entrepreneurs in exploiting their ideas and taking them to market.

Chapter 3: Research and Development and the Small Firm
The chapter investigates R&D in terms of spillovers and technology absorption, the measurement of R&D activity and these activities in small businesses. In relation to these aspects the chapter considers R&D activities in businesses according to demand, organisation, innovation, imitation and diffusion, complementary assets, networking and government influence on business R&D.

Chapter 4: Technology Diffusion
This chapter considers technology diffusion, technology transfer networks, a model of technology diffusion, "best practice" and implications for policy. Technology diffusion in the form of new or improved technology, the transmission of knowledge or technical expertise is investigated. This involves spillovers through formal and informal networks enabling learning by interacting and an absorptive capacity to assimilate new technology developed elsewhere. Implications for policy relevant to technology and entrepreneurship arising from the model are also investigated and conclusions are drawn.

Chapter 5: Clusters and Knowledge Flows
Clusters and knowledge flows are explored together with mobility within clusters followed by the example of the Inkjet Printing Cluster in the Cambridge area. Labour mobility and knowledge spillovers in clusters are interrelated phenomena with knowledge embodied in entrepreneurs and specialised workers can spill over from one enterprise to another through labour mobility and direct revelation (Guarino and Tedeschi, 2006). It is found that knowledge diffused by the mobility of employees contributes to a cluster performing better through the generation of spinouts and the accumulation of knowledge (Dahl, 2002).

Chapter 6: Higher Education Spin-offs
Academic entrepreneurs, academic spin-offs and the economic importance of academic spin-offs are explored in this chapter. A number of factors will influence the ability to establish and develop spin-offs. Some of these arise from the priorities and views of university researchers and characteristics of academic culture. Others are from the wider business environment and the ability of the academic-industry infrastructure to promote and support the development of spin-offs. Supply-side factors will include the business background, skills, relevant experience and access to finance, of the founders/co-founders of spin-offs. Whereas, the demand-side factors will include unemployment in the region, demand for the services provided by the spin-offs, the local industry structure (whether conducive to the formation of spin-offs), and the level of economic activity in the local economy.

Chapter 7: Global Start-ups and business development
This chapter examines the characteristics of global start-ups and relates case studies of these small businesses. By describing, understanding and interpreting the reasons behind the emergence of global start-ups it is possible to gain insight into their needs for business support. Six global start-up case studies are described, which were investigated, and these reveal different characteristics and aspects for business development. Perhaps the main limitation is that most of the companies are in the early stage of business development, but it is envisaged that this work will be developed into a longitudinal study which will show interesting evolutionary dynamics in future years.

Chapter 8: Innovation Performance Indicators
Innovation performance indicators and small firms are discussed together with an examination of innovation performance, a framework for measuring innovation performance and regional innovation performance. The extant concepts and research the chapter builds on is the recent work into innovation performance indicators, at national and regional levels. A framework for selecting and placing indicators in three performance areas is explored according to i) basic research and the production of new knowledge; ii) links between public and private research and iii) levels of industrial innovation (OECD, 2001). Through categorisation and weighting, indicators are determined to measure innovation performance.

Recommended Reading

Thomas, B. (2000) Triple Entrepreneurial Connection: Colleges, Government and Industry, London: Janus Publishing Company.

Thomas, B. and Simmons, G. (eds.) (2010) *E-Commerce Adoption and Small Business in the Global Marketplace: Tools for Optimization*, Business Science Reference, Hershey: IGI Global.

References

Allen, T., Hyman, D. and Pinckney, D. (1983) Transferring Technology to the Small Manufacturing Firm: A Study of Technology Transfer in Three Countries, *Research Policy*, 12(2), 199-211.

Asheim, B.T., Isaksen, A. (2002) Regional Innovation Systems: The Integration Of Local 'Sticky' And Global 'Ubiquitous' Knowledge, *Journal of Technology Transfer*, 27, 77-86.

Baregheh, A., Rowley, J. and Sambrook, S. (2009) Towards a multidisciplinary definition of innovation, *Management Decision*, 47(8), pp. 1323-1339.

Cheese, J. (1993) Sourcing technology - industry and higher education in Germany and the UK, *Industry and Higher Education*, March, 30-38.

Collins (1997) *Collins Concise Dictionary*, Glasgow, Harper Collins.

Cooke, P. (2001) *Strategies for Regional Innovation Systems: Learning Transfer and Applications*, UNIDO World Industrial Development Report (WIDR).

Dahl, M.S. (2002) Embedded Knowledge Flows through Labour Mobility in Regional Clusters in Denmark, Paper presented at the *DRIUD Summer Conference on "Industrial Dynamics of the New and Old Economy – who is embracing whom?"*, Copenhagen/Elsinore 6-8 June.

Desforges, C.D. (1985) USA/UK Experience in Technology Transfer: a comparative analysis, *CDP Conference on Commercial and Industrial Collaboration*, Sheffield, 27.

Doloreux, D. (2002) What we should know about regional systems of innovation, *Technology and Society*, 24, 243-263.

European Commission (EC) (1993) Growth, competitiveness, employment: the challenges and ways forward into the 21st Century, *Bulletin of the European Communities*, Supplement 6/93.

European Commission (EC) (1994) *Growth, competitiveness, employment: the challenges and ways forward into the 21st Century*, White Paper, Brussels, EC.

European Commission (EC) (2005) *The new SME definition - User guide and model declaration*, Enterprise and Industry Publications, Brussels: European Commission.

European Commission (EC) (2007) *Fourth European Community Innovation Survey: Strengths and Weaknesses of European Countries*, Brussels: European Commission.

Evangelista, R., Iammarino, S., Mastrostefano, V. and Silvani, A. (2002) 'Looking for regional systems of innovation: evidence from the Italian innovation survey', *Regional Studies*, 36(2), pp.173–186.

Guarino, A. and Tedeschi, P. (2006) *Endogenous Knowledge Spillovers and Labour Mobility in Industrial Clusters*, Department of Economics and ELSE, University College, London.

Lovering, J. (1999) Theory led by Policy: The Inadequacies of the "New Regionalism" (Illustrated from the Case of Wales), *International Journal for Urban and Regional Research*, 23(2), 379-395.

Martinussen, J. (1992) Business Creation and Technology Transfer, *OECD Seminar on Strategies for Promoting Technology Transfer*, Grenoble, April, 11.

Moulaert, F. and Sekia, F. (2003) Territorial innovation models: a critical survey, *Regional Studies*, 37, 289-302.

Organisation for Economic Co-operation and Development (OECD), 2001; *The New Economy: Beyond the Hype – The OECD Growth Project.*

Rothwell, R. (1994) The changing nature of the innovation process: implications for SMEs, in Oakey, R (ed.), *New Technology-Based Firms in the 1990s*, London, Paul Chapman, 11-21.

Saxenian, A. (1991) The Origins and Dynamics of Production Networks in Silicon Valley, *Research Policy*, 20, 423-437.

Thomas, M. and Rhisiart, M. (2000) Innovative Wales, Bryan, J. and Jones, C. (eds.) *Wales in the 21st Century: An Economic Future*, London, Macmillan Business, 115-122.

Uyarra, E. (2005) *Knowledge, Diversity and Regional Innovation Policies: Theoretical Issues and Empirical Evidence of Regional Innovation Strategies*, PREST Discussion Paper Series, Institute of Innovation Research, University of Manchester, Manchester, 1-18.

2. Invention, Innovation and Small Business

"Where a new invention promises to be useful, it ought to be tried"
                                                THOMAS JEFFERSON (1762-1826)

This chapter at a glance

- Introduction
- Distinction between invention and innovation
- The Interrelationships between invention, innovation and small business
- Conclusions

Introduction

Much has been written about invention and inventive activity – and today increasingly, about the concept of 'entrepreneurship'. Published work typically describes inventive activity on a historical-developmental basis or as a collection of case studies, presenting qualitative findings in relation to the inventive developments taking place. Indeed, the relationship between invention, innovation and entrepreneurship has involved much discussion. Innovation is defined by Kanter (1983) as involving 'creative use as well as original invention' and simply it is defined by Mellor (2005) as 'creativity plus application' or 'invention plus application'. According to Porter (1990) 'invention and entrepreneurship are at the heart of national advantage' and Burns (2007) reports that 'invention is the extreme and riskiest form of innovation'. In particular, Bolton and Thompson (2000) highlight creativity in the invention and innovation process and Burns (2007) posits that 'invention can be successfully exploited in the entrepreneurial environment'.

The inter-relationship between invention, innovation and entrepreneurship is both of theoretical and practical significance. It may involve inventors and entrepreneurs in all aspects of the process of product, process or service development but also it can involve them separately. The latter case is exemplified historically by Adam Smith (1776) who observed that 'all the improvements in machinery, however, have by no means been the inventions of those who had occasion to use the machines'. He also considered the way in which the division of labour promoted specialised inventions. This is articulated by Marx (1858) who notes 'invention then becomes a branch of business, and the application of science to immediate production aims at determining the inventions at the same time as it solicits them'. Freeman and Soete (1997, p.15) develop this theme of invention as 'an essential condition of economic progress and a critical element in the competitive struggle of enterprises and of nation-states'. And that it 'is of importance not only for increasing the wealth of nations in the narrow sense of increased prosperity, but also in the more fundamental sense of enabling men (and women) to do things which have never been done before at all. It enables the whole quality of life to be changed for better or for worse. It can mean not merely more of the same goods but a pattern of goods and services which has not previously existed, except in the imagination'.

Freeman and Soete (1997, p.16) remark that 'although most economists have made a deferential nod in the direction of technological change, few have stopped to examine it'. This paradox has been explained by Jewkes at al (1969) in terms of the ignorance of science and technology by economists, their pre-occupation with the trade cycle and employment problems, and limited statistics. This was demonstrated by Jewkes et al (1969) in their study of 'The Sources of Invention' and has been confirmed before and since by empirical studies. Freeman and Soete (1997, p.17) develop this argument regarding the neglect of invention since it 'was not only due to other pre-occupations of economists nor to their ignorance of technology; they were also the victims of their own assumptions and commitment to accepted systems of thought. These tended to treat the flow of new knowledge, of inventions.... as outside the framework of economic models, or more strictly, as 'exogenous variables''.

Distinction between invention and innovation

The distinction between invention and innovation was originally owed to Schumpeter (1934, 1961) and has since become part of economic theory. Freeman and Soete (1997, p.22) add, 'an invention is an idea, a sketch or a model for a new improved device, product, process or system. Such inventions may often (not always) be patented but they do not necessarily lead to technical innovations'. Also, 'the chain of events from invention or specification to social application is often longer and hazardous' (Freeman and Soete, 1997, p.22). The crucial role of the entrepreneur in this complex process was recognised by Schumpeter (1934, 1961), although he did not consider the study of invention to be of significance in itself. He stressed that the decision of the entrepreneur to commercialise an invention was the decisive step and defined the entrepreneur as the 'innovator'. A summary of the inputs and outputs of this process, based on Ames (1961) and Freeman and Soete (1997) is presented in Table 2.1.

Process	Inventive inputs		Inventive outputs	
	Feedback Inputs from	Other inputs	Feedback output	Other outputs
Inventive work	Orders from entrepreneurs Inventive work development	Outputs of research	New technological problems Unexplainable successes and failures	Patents Non-patentable inventions

Table 2.1: Inputs and outputs of Inventive work

Adapted from: Ames (1961) and Freeman and Soete (1997)

In the nineteenth century inventor-entrepreneurs or individual inventors established new firms to develop and exploit processes which they had invented or helped to invent. During the 19th century and before that time invention was likely to have been carried out in geographical and social isolation through 'like minds' working on a similar problem (Blaikie, 1993; Naughton, 2007). The significance of the inventor-entrepreneur is noted by Radosevich (1995) and Djokovic and Souitaris (2004). Following this in the twentieth century, according to Freeman and Soete (1997), there was a shift towards large-scale corporate research and development (R&D). This is contrary to the interpretation provided by Jewkes et al (1969) in their classic study 'The Sources of Invention', as already mentioned. In this, they reduce the difference between the nineteenth and twentieth centuries and minimise the importance of corporate R&D. Moreover, they argued that important twentieth century inventions were the result of individual inventors similar to the nineteenth century. Inventors 'free-lancing' or working in universities achieved this. In fact, they concede that due to the extortionate development costs, large-scale corporations will often still be necessary to bring inventions into commercial exploitation. Indeed, out of 64 major twentieth century inventions, 40 were attributed to individual inventors compared to 24 from corporate R&D, and out of the 40 half of these were dependent for commercial development on large firms.

Freeman and Soete (1997) maintained from the standpoint of economics that it was innovation that was of central interest rather than invention. Although, they did not deny the importance of invention, or the vital contribution creative individuals make to invention. This has been highlighted by Johnson (1975) who recognised the economic significance of invention itself in terms of its process and relationship, to the size of the firm and the role of the individual inventor. Freeman and Soete (1997) see no inconsistency between Jewkes et al's emphasis on the importance of university research and invention and the interpretation they give. (The interaction of the inventor with universities has more recently been noted by Agrawal (2001) in terms of university-to-industry knowledge transfer). Nor do they deny that the 'lone wolf' and the 'inventor-entrepreneur' still play an important role. But they do note even on Jewkes et al's account of major inventions, that there has been a shift since the early twentieth century to a larger contribution from inventors associated with corporate R&D. Although the difference between nineteenth and twentieth century invention cannot be lightly dismissed a new pattern began to emerge in the twentieth century, in which the role of the inventor-entrepreneur became less important. Whereas the UK is perceived as being a nation of inventors (HM Treasury, 2004) it appears that the principal way to be successful commercially today is to be an 'entrepreneurial inventor' (Nicholas, 2003).

According to Freeman and Soete (1997, p.169) 'the test of successful entrepreneurship and good management is the capacity to link together.... technical and market possibilities.... Innovation is a coupling process and the coupling first takes place in the minds of imaginative people.... But once the idea has 'clicked' in the mind of the inventor or entrepreneur, there is still a long way to go before it becomes a successful innovation.... The one-(person) inventor-entrepreneur.... may very much simplify this process in the early stages of a new innovating firm, but in the later stages and in any established firm the 'coupling' process involves linking and co-ordinating different sections, departments and individuals.'

The Interrelationships between invention, innovation and small business

A fundamental question regarding the role of the individual inventor is whether invention depends on individual inventors in terms of national and regional policies, which may aim to liberate individual 'inventiveness'. According to Norris and Vaizey (1973) this widely held view may be false. It is debatable whether this is the case since although most inventions are promulgated by individuals, due to a creative idea emerging from one person, it is possible for two or more people to get together to formulate an idea. This is contrary to Norris and Vaizey's assertion that 'groups of people do not tend to produce creative ideas' (Norris and Vaizey, 1973, p.36). This leads to the possibility of co-invention and this is supported by the research reported by Thomas et al (2009) in a survey of inventors which provides evidence of inventors working together in a number of cases. Contrary to this, although inventors may work together, it is still the case that many will be individual inventors, nevertheless but not exclusively.

This leads to a number of possibilities regarding invention. Not only will there be individual and co-inventors, there will also be serial inventors (developing inventions one after another) and parallel inventors (developing a number of ideas at the same time). Ideas developed at any time may be linked or they may be separate. When exploring what is meant by 'individual inventor' Norris and Vaizey (1973) contend that there are two principal types. In the first sense, an individual inventor is someone who works by themselves (otherwise known as a 'lone inventor'), determining the direction of the work and financing the activity from their own resources. The results of the work will remain with the individual at this stage of development. In these terms, inventive activity will probably be carried out on a part-time basis or as a 'leisure' pursuit of someone employed. At the other end of the scale the corporate or institutional inventor may be a core tenured employee who is working in a specific area the results of which will be retained by the employer. Located between these two there will be many variations. Between the individual inventor and the corporate inventor there will be individuals who have characteristics of both. It will be a matter of judgement whether these are described as individual inventors. The relationships between invention, innovation and entrepreneurship, inventors, innovators and entrepreneurs, and micro, small and medium-sized enterprises (SMEs) and large corporations are illustrated in Table 2.2. There is also the distinction between profit orientation and societal orientation of entrepreneurs and entrepreneurship, but the latter has been excluded from this study due to being a discrete research investigation in itself.

Activity/Level	Invention	Innovation	Entrepreneurship
Micro	Individual/lone inventor	Innovator	Entrepreneur
Small and medium-sized enterprise	Company inventor	Innovation champions	Entrepreneur/ intrapreneur
Large company or organisation	Institutional/ Corporate inventor	Project champions	Intrapreneur

Table 2.2: The inter-relationships between invention, innovation and entrepreneurship
Source: Thomas and Gornall (2002)

The measurement of the relative magnitude of inventive activity by inventors is problematic due to the absence of expenditure on this type of activity. As a consequence, measurement is currently based purely on outcomes. The two main sources of information are therefore patent statistics and information on significant inventions. According to Kuznets (1962) there are four possible dimensions to an invention - a technical and an economic magnitude, and a past and a future. The technical past relates to the magnitude of the technical problem resolved by the invention. Consequently, some inventions are of a greater magnitude than others. The technical future can be measured according to the size of the invention, which is dependent on the inventions that follow. The economic past of an invention involves the cost and is measured according to the resources used. Lastly, the economic future of an invention involves the production of new goods or services and can enable cost reductions.

Although the above measures act as a conceptual framework, it remains an educated guess to determine the difference between significant and insignificant inventions. Jewkes et al (1969) in their work on the most important inventions in the twentieth century, as already described, assembled a list in their judgement of the most significant inventions. Out of these, as well as individual inventors, there was evidence that universities and government research laboratories produced a considerable number of inventions too. Factors affecting the individual inventor as a major source of invention include time, 'atmosphere', finance and technological resources. The complexities of finding finance by an inventor are explored by Hobbs (2006) in terms of the inventor-investor relationship.

With regard to time, small businesses will be interested in inventions that will yield a pay-off within a short period of time and many firms will expect expenditures to be paid off within five years (Norris and Vaizey, 1973; Freeman and Soete, 1997). Since five years will have to include the process of recouping spending on research, invention, innovation and marketing, this will restrict the magnitude of the scale of the advancement of knowledge. As a consequence, most company R&D is concerned with small improvements.

In a small business context, a factor working against invention is the problem of providing the right 'atmosphere'. Another major factor working against the individual inventor is the lack of finance and this is why they appear to have declined in importance in the twentieth century. Much invention will also require specialised technological equipment with a cost beyond the reach of many individual inventors. It could therefore be expected that the role of the individual inventor would be most significant in areas which do not need large amounts of expensive technological equipment. Norris and Vaizey (1973) state that since inventions can be a result of many highly trained personnel working methodically on problems with considerable financial backing, it is clearly the case that there can be both contentions that inventions have been the result of both team and individual work. They therefore surmise that the individual inventor will continue to play a significant role.

According to Spence (1995) innovation is often used to indicate something new, created or produced and it is commonly confused with invention. Whereas inventions can be seen as innovations because they are new, innovations are not necessarily inventions. Spence (1995) further says that innovations may be long-established ideas, products or services involving a new application and consequently may be considered novel. An interesting development of the classic distinction between innovation and invention is with regard to technical novelties (McKelvey, 1997). These may be hidden in an inventor's garage or in a research and development (R&D) department. They may also be mentioned in patents but remain unused, developed or sold and are therefore technical inventions. As technical novelties, they include a combination of techniques and knowledge, and technologies. In fact, inventions become innovations when they are used for marketable products or sold. Indeed, many innovations will have a degree of technical novelty and involve interaction with the market place.

'Collective invention' 'is the free exchange of information about new techniques and plant designs among actual and potential competitors' (Foray, 1997). This has been described in the case of the iron industry: 'If a firm constructed a new plant of novel design and that plant proved to have lower costs than other plants, these facts were made available to other firms in the industry and to potential entrants. The next firm constructing a new plant could build on the experience of the first by introducing and extending the design change that had proved profitable. The operating characteristics of this second plant would then also be made available to potential investors. In this way fruitful lines of technical advance were identified and pursued.' (Allen, 1983, p.2) It is through this behaviour that cumulative advance takes place (Ehrnberg and Jacobsson, 1997).

It appears that individual entrepreneurship has become less important and collective entrepreneurship more important (Edquist and Johnson, 1997). Radosevic (1997) has identified 'enterprization' which is the process of building complete enterprises instead of production units (Jacobsson, 1997). The term was originally coined by Bornsel (1994). The proposition therefore is that there are not only explicit factors involved in the process of individual invention, as described in the literature, but also implicit factors including personal characteristics.

Conclusions

The fundamental difference that differentiates an inventor from an entrepreneur is that an inventor will develop a new product or service, but may not take it to market. Whereas an entrepreneur will take the risk of bringing together resources to take a good or service to market with the intention of making a profit (Gallagher and Hopkins, 1999). Indeed, the entrepreneur may not be an inventor and not all inventors are entrepreneurs. Moreover, innovation is the interaction of an invention into a use that has economic value. This will be what the entrepreneur adds. Inventors will design and develop new products and services and entrepreneurs will recognise the opportunities (Burns, 2007), take the risk of starting a small business, and accept the challenges. It should also be remembered that inventions solve problems and will lead to other inventions.

Recommended Reading

Thomas, B., Gornall, L., Packham, G. and Miller, C. (2009) The individual inventor and the implications for innovation and entrepreneurship, *Industry and Higher Education*, 23(5), pp. 391-403.

References

Agrawal, A. (2001) University-to-industry knowledge transfer: literature review and unanswered questions, *International Journal of Management Reviews*, 3(4), pp. 285-302.

Allen, R.C. (1983) 'Collective invention', Journal of Economic Behaviour and Economic Organization, 4, pp.1-24.

Ames, E. (1961) 'Research, invention, development and innovation', *American Economic Review*, 51(3), pp.370-81.

Blaikie, N. (1993) *Approaches to Social Enquiry*, Blackwell Publishers, Cambridge, USA.

Bolton, B. and Thompson, J. (2000) *Entrepreneurs: Talent, Temperament, Technique*, Butterworth-Heinemann, Oxford.

Bornsel, O. (1994) 'Enjeux industriels du post-socialisme', Cahier de Recherche 94 – C – 2, CERNA, Écoles des Mines, Colloque de l'Association Française de Science Economique, Paris, September.

Burns, P. (2007) *Entrepreneurship and Small Business*, Palgrave Macmillan, Basingstoke.

Djokovic, D. and Souitaris, V. (2004) *Spinouts from Academic Institutions: A Literature Review with suggestions for further research*, Faculty of Management, Cass Business School, City University, London.

Edquist, C. and Johnson, B. (1997) 'Institutions and Organizations in Systems of Innovation' in Edquist, C. (ed) *Systems of Innovation: Technologies, Institutions and Organizations*, Pinter, London, p.53.

Ehrnberg, E. and Jacobsson, S. (1997) 'Technological Discontinuities and Incumbents' Performance: An Analytical Framework' in Edquist, C. (ed) *Systems of Innovation: Technologies, Institutions and Organizations*, Pinter, London, pp.318-341.

Foray, D. (1997) 'Generation and Distribution of Technological Knowledge: Incentives, Norms, and Institutions' in Edquist, C. (ed) *Systems of Innovation: Technologies, Institutions and Organizations*, Pinter, London, p.73.

Freeman, C. and Soete, L. (1997) *The Economics of Industrial Innovation*, 3rd edn, Pinter, London.

Gallagher, S. and Hopkins, M. (1999) 'US History: Inventors and Entrepreneurs' *EconEd Link*, http://www.econedlink.org/.

HM Treasury (2004) Department of Trade and Industry and Department for Education and Skills, *Science and Innovation: Working Towards a Ten-Year Investment Framework*, HM Treasury, London, March.

Hobbs, F. (2006) The inventor-investor conundrum, *Industry and Higher Education*, 20(6), December, pp.381-385.

Jacobsson, S. (1997) 'Systems Transformation: Technological and Institutional Change' in Edquist, C. (ed) *Systems of Innovation: Technologies and Organizations*, Pinter, London, p.296.

Jewkes, J., Sawers, D. and Stillerman, R. (1969) *The Sources of Invention*, 2nd end, Macmillan, London.

Johnson, P.S. (1975) *The Economics of Invention and Innovation*, Martin Robertson, London, pp. 29-50, 51-71 and 244-250.

Kanter, R.M. (1983) The Change Masters: Innovation and Productivity in American Corporations, Simon and Schuster, New York.

Kirakowski, J. (2000) *Questionnaires in Usability Engineering*, Human Factors Research Group, Cork, Ireland.

Kuznets, S. (1962) *'Inventive activity: problems of definition and measurement'*, National Bureau Committee for Economic Research, The Rate and Direction of Inventive Activity, Princeton University Press, Princeton.

Marx, K. (1858) *Grundrisse*, Allen Lane edn, London, 1973.

McKelvey, M. (1997) 'Using Evolutionary Theory to Define Systems of Innovation' in Edquist, C. (ed) *Systems of Innovation: Technologies, Institutions and Organizations*, Pinter, London, p.201.

Mellor, R.B. (2005) Sources and Spread of Innovation in Small e-Commerce Companies, Forlaget Globe, Skodsborgvej.

Naughton, R. (2007) *Adverntures in Cybersound*, Project Report: Literature Review, SS705 Research Methods, http://www.acmi.net.au/AIC/phd6000_lit.html (accessed 23/01/2007).

Nicholas, D. (2003) The Virtual Company (TVC), *Inventique*, (Newsletter of the Wessex Round Table of Inventors), No. 30, March.

Norris, K. and Vaizey, J. (1973) *The Economics of Research and Technology*, George Allen & Unwin, London, pp.36-42.

Porter, M.E. (1990) *The Competitive Advantage of Nations*, Free Press, New York.

Radosevic, S. (1997) 'Systems of Innovation in Transformation: From Socialism to Post-Socialism' in Edquist, C. (ed) *Systems of Innovation: Technologies, Institutions and Organizations*, Pinter, London, p.379.

Radosevich, R. (1995) A model for entrepreneurial spin-offs from public technology sources, *International Journal of Technology Management*, 10(7-8), pp. 879-893.

Schumpeter, J. (1934) *The Theory of Economic Development*, Harvard University Press, Massachusetts, USA.

Schumpeter, J. (1961) *The Theory of Economic Development*, Oxford University Press, first edn, Oxford, 1934.

Smith, A. (1776) An Inquiry into the Nature and Causes of the Wealth of Nations, Dent edn 1910, London, p.8.

Spence, W.R. (1995) Innovation: The Communication of Change in Ideas, Practices and Products, Chapman & Hall, London, p.4.

Thomas, B. and Gornall, L. (2002) The Role of the Individual Inventor and the implications for Innovation and Entrepreneurship – A View from Wales, *25th ISBA National Small Firms Policy and Research Conference: Competing Perspectives of Small Business and Entrepreneurship*, Brighton, 13th-15th November.

3. Research and Development and the Small Firm

"The practice of R&D involves making mistakes, realizations, corrections, and more mistakes. ..."
TOM HUFF (1943-)

This chapter at a glance

- Introduction
- Spillovers from R&D
- Technology Absorption and R&D
- Measuring R&D activity
- R&D activities in small businesses
- Conclusions

Introduction

This chapter considers Research and Development (R&D) in terms of spillovers and technology absorption. According to Revesz and Boldeman (2006) the economic reason for governments to support R&D is based upon the externalities (spillovers) caused by R&D which has received much interest in innovation literature. Further to this two roles for R&D suggested by Griffith et al (2004) are to stimulate innovation and to create an understanding of discoveries by others which to the originating firm are confidential. A major policy question concerning R&D will be the extent to which indigenous technology progress involving small business is created by local R&D or by developments globally (Revesz and Boldeman, 2006). It must be borne in mind that economic growth can be created through assimilated disembodied knowledge (education, learning, R&D, knowledge systems and economic reform) contrary to the embodiment of technology innovations in imports (DCITA, 2005).

Spillovers from R&D

It has already been recognised that the technological development of indigenous enterprises is influenced by various sources of know-how including R&D, industry contacts, learning, ICT and publications. R&D is therefore a major source for technological progress in a modern economy. A principal justification for government support of R&D policy activities will rest upon the positive spillovers which are the positive externalities from R&D (Revesz and Boldeman, 2006).

The Schumpeterian hypothesis (1934; 1942) suggests market concentration and large production units for R&D intensive industries are not necessarily confirmed through empirical evidence. Whereas in R&D intensive industries there will be a tendency to industrial concentration at a global level (small firms will exist as suppliers of components and as "niche" product competitors), in other R&D intensive industries there will be numerous small enterprises of niche products (Revesz and Boldman, 2006). The process of "creative destruction" (Schumpeter, 1934; 1942) means that enterprises in technology dynamic industries, where there is oligopolistic competition, will need to innovate to maintain their position in the market. Caballero and Jaffe (1993) have provided empirical support for this hypothesis and according to Nelson (1990) the views of R&D and company managers also support this point.

Levin et al (1987) in a survey of large corporations in the United States examined a number of methods used by enterprises to protect the competitive advantage of new or improved processes and products and these were patents, secrecy, lead time, moving quickly along the learning curve and sales and service. With "first mover advantage" it was found that secrecy was the most widely used method to protect intellectual property (IP) in industry (Arundel, 2001). Since small "outsider" enterprises in markets controlled by oligopolies will often need patents in order to release new products they will often licence production to a larger firm (Mazzoleni and Nelson, 1998). Innovation surveys have found similar results, for example the survey reported by Phillips (1997). Also, in some sectors functions of patents can be replaced by copyright (Revesz, 1999). Once knowledge is created and due to non-exclusion it is hard to stop others using it and to keep private and this is the non-appropriation problem (Revesz and Boldeman, 2006). In relation to this Quah (2003) has considered with regard to the information society the public good aspects. Further to this with knowledge there is the implication of only charging for marginal dissemination costs (Arrow, 1962). As a result additional learning costs will be incurred by the user when making use of this knowledge (Mandeville, 1998). It could be suggested that since the market provides the means for appropriating innovation benefits there will be no need for supplementation through government intervention in the form of IP protection and R&D subsidies since oligopoly market conditions will be apparent in R&D intensive service industries and manufacturing (Mandeville et al, 1982). In particular, on a qualitative basis there will be the case both pro and ante for R&D government support and quantitative analysis will be required in order to determine R&D subsidies at an optimum level (Revesz and Boldeman, 2006).

Whereas scientific knowledge (mostly public sector R&D) which contributes to greater understanding instead of new applications in the public domain is more available know-how and technical information ("proprietary" knowledge) tends not to be publicised and surveys of R&D and business managers have supported this view that patent disclosures and technical publications do not play a significant role in the provision of technology information to innovative enterprises (Revesz and Boldeman, 2006). Indeed, a survey in the United States by Schuchman (1981) found that engineers involved with new technologies relied on in-house expertise and talking to colleagues for information that was relevant and they tended not to use technical publications. Further to this, Taylor and Silbertson (1973) considered how much R&D managers in the UK would pay if access to abstracts and patent records was denied.

A number of surveys have been undertaken to consider the time delay and cost in the imitation of inventions (Revesz and Boldeman, 2006). For example, more than one hundred and twenty respondents to a survey (mostly United States R&D executives) were asked by Levin et al (1987) for an estimation of time and costs needed to copy innovations by a competitor and it was found that in less than 5 years most inventions could be imitated. Similarly, Mansfield (1981; 1985) revealed that reverse engineering, personal contacts and the movement of staff between companies were the principal sources of the leakages of information.

Technology Absorption and R&D

According to Griffith et al (2004), two roles for R&D are those of (i) stimulating innovation and (ii) enabling understanding and the imitation of discoveries which remain confidential by other originating firms. R&D therefore plays an important role for the development of an "absorptive capacity" and is equally critical for technology transfer and innovation (Revesz and Boldeman, 2006). Econometric evidence concerning the importance of the "two faces of R&D" are also presented by Griffith et al (2004) through the examination of productivity growth in industries for 12 OECD economies. R&D appears to stimulate innovation indirectly by technology transfer or directly by those involved with leading edge technology frontiers (Revesz and Boldeman, 2006). Further, it is suggested that R&D plays a crucial role in multi factor productivity levels for industries in OECD countries (Griffith et al, 2004). Cohen and Levinthal (1989) have provided a similar view about the importance of R&D in nurturing both learning and innovation. In particular the importance of R&D in enhancing technology absorption is considered important for small businesses.

With regard to patents it is perceived that there are advantages in reducing patent monopolies by limiting protection or reducing duration (Scotchmer, 2004; Mazzoleni and Nelson; 1998 and Revesz, 1999). There can also be a reluctance to seek strong protection for patents (Scotchmer, 2004; Mandeville et al, 1982; Mazzoleni and Nelson, 1998). Before spillover benefits are known it is difficult to estimate these for R&D projects (Allen Consulting, 2005). Michael Polanyi (1943) suggested the replacement of patent monopolies with the government control of invention licensing rights by an expert industry panel awarding the inventor.

Public support schemes for R&D activities, although very often exhibiting problems, can be run with an acceptable level of difficulties and these can include subsidies for business R&D, research by public bodies (especially universities) and IP protection (Revesz and Boldeman, 2006). The level of government support for innovation can be difficult to gauge especially since there is limited information on R&D activity and there may be a number of policy options (Scotchmer, 2004).

Measuring R&D activity

Although there appears to be no data on the commercial return from R&D activities, case studies of firm managers show that they will invest in R&D due to competitor's technology advances and the fear of being out of business (Revesz and Boldeman, 2006). In a study by Revesz and Lattimore (2001) no statistical positive significance between R&D intensity and firm profitability was found and a survey by Jaruzelski et al (2005) also found no direct relationship between R&D spending and corporate success. It is generally agreed that at international and national levels R&D spillovers are considerable and are many times greater than private returns (Lederman and Maloney, 2003; Sena, 2004). Studies on the economic impact of R&D have focused on the rate of return for business R&D at national levels (Maddock, 2002; Shanks and Zheng, 2006).

A major problem when trying to measure R&D activity is that it is a concept based upon definitions and represents activities in the area of scientific and technological acquisition by organisations and enterprises (Revesz and Boldeman, 2006). Statistical agencies in industrialised countries use the Frascati Manual definitions for R&D activity (OECD, 2002). The definition of R&D by the OECD is:

"Research and experimental development (R&D) comprise creative work undertaken on a systematic basis in order to increase the stock of knowledge, including knowledge of man, culture and society, and the use of this stock of knowledge to devise new applications." (OECD, 2002)

A further definitional measurement problem is that it is difficult to determine the change in R&D activity arising from policy change.

Simple cost reduction measurement was followed by early research into the impact of R&D on productivity (Revesz and Boldeman, 2006). A pioneering study was undertaken by Grilliches (1957) involving a cost benefit analysis of the development of hybrid corn varieties in United States government research stations. Case studies undertaken on cost reductions from R&D in certain areas have provided interesting results (Revesz and Boldeman, 2006). Bresnahan (1986) considered consumer surplus through cost reductions in financial services arising from mainframe computers between 1958 and 1972 in the United States. Trajtenberg (1990), in a case study of computerised tomography scanners, found the rate of return to R&D in the United States to be 270% a year. The rate of return to business R&D was examined by Mansfield et al (1977) using several case studies in the United States. Unfortunately a major drawback of case studies is that they only consider innovations that are successful (Revesz and Boldeman, 2006). Alternatively, case studies can be useful when information about R&D costs and outcomes, which are commercially sensitive, is available from private businesses.

Estimation of knowledge spillovers was considered to be the main challenge for economic analysis of R&D by Grilliches (1992). A number of measures have been propounded for technology knowledge flows and these include the proximity in industrial or research field classification, statistics on foreign direct investment (FDI), statistics on licence fees and royalties, data on foreign trade, input and output linkages across sectors, citations on patents and patent registrations (Eaton and Kortum, 1996, 1999; Mohnen, 1996; Grilliches, 1992). According to Jaffe and Trajtenberg (1998) and Jaffe et al (1993) patent citations appear to be the best approach to determine knowledge flows between industries, regions and countries. Internal R&D can be measured by country (macro), sector (meso) or firm (micro) and external R&D similarly (external R&D indicators can be determined by R&D stocks or external sources and weighted by knowledge flow indicators – patent statistics, for example) (Revesz and Boldeman, 2006). Grilliches (1992) argued that the rate of depreciation of knowledge is quicker at the micro level than at the macro level. Statistical evidence on the obsolescence of R&D capital at the micro level in a technology competitive and dynamic environment supports the depreciation of knowledge supported by Schumpeter's (1934; 1942) creative destruction (Caballero and Jaffe, 1993).

Many R&D studies have only considered manufacturing since it represents the largest spend on R&D than any other sector (Revesz and Boldeman, 2006). The cost savings for 12 manufacturing sectors in the United States were estimated by Nadiri and Theofanis (1994) - the social manufacturing rate of return on public R&D was found to be between six and nine per cent by adding the marginal cost savings estimates. The rate companies registered significant product innovations and patents across technology fields in the United States was analysed by Acs et al (1994) who found that own R&D activity was important for large businesses who ran their own laboratories whereas smaller businesses benefited from publicly funded research knowledge (effectiveness of public research appeared to be enhanced by universities near to private sector research laboratories). Similar results were found by Audretsch and Vivarelli (1996) when investigating patenting activity for 15 Italian regions (own R&D was important for large businesses and regional university scientific research activity). The productivity growth rate in eighteen United States manufacturing sectors between 1953 and 1983 was related to the rate of publication of scientific papers for 9 scientific fields by Adams (1990) (productivity growth was found to be dependent on accumulated field specific scientific research and on industry employment in appropriate fields for scientists). The relationship between the size of R&D activity and the science base for 14 United States R&D sectors between 1961 and 1986 was examined by Adams (1993). He found that the size of the scientific base had a significant positive impact on R&D activity levels. R&D in universities has the important aim to provide post graduate students with research skills and related to this public R&D impulses considerable knowledge spillovers to business through "tacit" knowledge, training of researchers, collaborative ventures, resolving technological dilemmas and scientific and new discoveries (Revesz and Boldeman, 2006).

Whereas Lederman and Maloney (2003) found a relationship that was strongly negative for GDP per capita and national R&D intensity Gittleman and Wolff (1998) found that R&D intensity was positively related to the growth of gross domestic product (GDP) in advanced industrialised countries which infers that R&D is advantageous to countries with industries near to the frontiers of leading edge technologies. A significant policy question for R&D activity is to what extent domestic technology progress is influenced by global developments or domestic R&D (if this is by overseas technology progress there is the argument that there may be little need to foster domestic R&D).

Further to the Coe and Helpman (1995) model for cross border knowledge spillovers Eaton and Kortum (1996; 1999) considered the flow of ideas from abroad as well as those internally generated. Ideas from a country will depend on R&D sector productivity and size, the technological level, cross country patent applications and the use of these ideas by the country and other countries (Revesz and Boldeman, 2006). Pottelsberghe and Lichtenberg (2001) developed the Coe and Helpman (1995) model by including R&D stocks related to outward and inward investment in addition to the R&D content of imports. It is apparent that it is not possible to simply import overseas technologies since their application by local enterprises will require investment in learning involving R&D. Hirsch-Kreinsen et al (2005) observe that for medium low and low tech manufacturing firms the main source of innovation will not come from R&D but from other activities involving assimilation and learning such as contact with people in businesses in the same industry, suppliers and customers. It appears that most innovations in more than ninety per cent of an economy, excluding high and medium tech manufacturing, will not be through indigenous R&D (Revesz and Boldeman, 2006).

R&D activities in small businesses

Introduction

It has been found that R&D does not provide a true picture of innovation in SMEs since smaller enterprises will not have a specialist R&D department (Crespi et al, 2003). Further to this it appears that most innovations originate in certain sectors (Robson et al, 1988) as likewise most R&D (Scherer, 1982). In relation to these aspects this review considers R&D activities in small businesses according to demand, organisation, innovation, imitation and diffusion, complementary assets, networking and government influence on small business R&D.

Demand

With regard to demand it is apparent that the motivation to undertake R&D has involved variables representing market demand conditions which present demand as a major influence on such decisions (Crespi et al, 2003). Unfortunately, as noted by Mowery and Rosenberg (1979) this does not convey much since managers or entrepreneurs will consider the demand outcome before undertaking the development process which is likely to be expensive.

Organisation

According to the Schumpeterian perspective innovation and R&D activities in modern times have required large firms or concentrated industries (Crespi et al, 2003). Consequently, there will be sectors where the spend on R&D will be determined by the minimum operation scale but there will be other sectors where concentration will be in small and medium sized enterprises (SMEs) (Acs and Audretsch (1990) and Audretsch (1995) explain this according to different technological régimes across the different sectors and firm size). Acs and Audretsch (1990) further describe the differences in innovative activity between small and large firms according to the R&D intensities gap. Cohen (1995) notes that the scale economies in R&D may be a possible explanation for the impact of large sized firms. Contrary to this there may be diseconomies with larger firms and as a result government focus in many economies has changed to considering SMEs (Crespi et al, 2003). Further, data on small businesses has tended to underestimate their R&D effort (Tidd et al, 2001). According to von Tunzelmann (1995) all productive units involve the four functions of administration and finance, products, production processes and technology (with augmentation by R&D). In the literature on scale economies in R&D there is justification for merging large high technology firms (Fisher and Temin, 1973; Kohn and Scott, 1982) and in a literature survey by Martin et al (2003) it is shown that for scale economies in university research at team level scale economies are usually obtained by teams of between five and nine people in a subject. Economies in R&D will involve merging diverse technological fields for production and cost advantages (Crespi et al, 2003). Contrary to examples of fusion that are successful there will also be cases where fusion has not been successful in a company (Kodama, 1991). The cycle time is the speed for R&D to be turned into new products and in order to be first to market there will be pressure for small businesses to shorten the time (Crespi et al, 2003). Taking aside increase in complexity a faster cycle time has its own costs (Scherer and Ross, 1990).

Innovation, imitation and diffusion

Ownership of innovation and intellectual property rights (IPRs) will be fundamental to determine the attractiveness to carry out R&D. Recent studies, however, have suggested that R&D is often undertaken in ways that appear more like imitation than innovation (Crespi et al, 2003). Indeed, the work of Cohen and Levinthal (1989, 1990) highlight absorptive capacity which they describe as the capacity to absorb technologies which are generated elsewhere. They contend that R&D increases absorption even if the R&D is not innovative but rather duplicative.

Complementary assets

Within enterprises there is a danger that there will be too narrow focus on innovation and R&D since as well as the ability to create new products and processes absorptive capacity will depend on the other resources and functions within and outside the organisation (Crespi et al, 2003). Teece (1986) has called these other resources complementary assets. In relation to this Dodgson and Rothwell (1994) have purported that SMEs will be likely to encounter difficulties translating external opportunities due to limited internal capabilities. According to many studies a significant determinant of R&D in SMEs appears to be financing of innovation and the role of cash flow (Crespi et al, 2003). In the literature on appropriate methods for the evaluation of the financing of R&D Myers (1984) has suggested options valuations instead of payback procedures or conventional discounted cash flow (DCF). A problem is that if a company leaves an R&D project it may be far more expensive to return at a later date (Mitchell and Hamilton, 1988). Marketing functions also need to be taken into account since there may be a considerable gulf between marketing and R&D (Crespi et al, 2003). Most studies have found a positive connection between R&D intensity and diversification and recent research shows that when the share of external contracted out R&D rises this leads to higher returns (Bönte, 2003).

Networking

Industries have always depended on sources external to the company for technologies for R&D and some of those that have had in-house R&D in recent times have externalised part of the function (Crespi et al, 2003). The performance of R&D in the UK by higher education institutions (HEIs) has increased from a figure below similar countries in 1980 to the same as similar nations (von Tunzelmann, 2004). It is thought that this has arisen due to the triple helix of activities between government, industry and universities (Etzkowitz and Leydesdorff, 2002). It appears that the interrelationship between HEIs and industry is a significant driver regarding the intensity of R&D (Crespi et al, 2003).

Government influence on business R&D

There are a number of ways government activities can influence business R&D and these include basic research funding, industrial R&D finance (by the tax system indirectly or directly) and through IPR. Gains in technological achievements through more R&D and patents can be caused by rising Gross Domestic Product (GDP) and other macroeconomic forces (von Tunzelmann and Efendioglu, 2001). Indeed, surveys of business R&D have revealed that a strong incentive is a macro economy in a buoyant situation (von Tunzelmann, 2003). Furthermore, governments see their contribution to technology from pump priming basic research funding with an emphasis on basic research arising from market failure (funding will contribute to business R&D through the subsidisation of private sector laboratories and spillovers complementing private R&D) (Crespi et al, 2003). There has also been concern since the 1980s over private sector R&D being crowded out by government R&D (Kealey, 1996; David et al, 2000). Other studies in the UK have suggested that increases in government R&D in defence activities resulted in skilled researchers being drawn away from commercialisable and private R&D (Walker, 1980). A study by von Tunzelmann and Efendioglu (2001) of the cross country effects of interest rates on R&D since the 1960s provided a positive long term correlation.

Governments can influence the level of R&D expenditures by small firms in two principal ways and these are by offering fiscal incentives or by directly subsidising such expenditures (an OECD survey in 2002 showed that in order to encourage business R&D countries have used fiscal incentives and these have involved tax deferrals, allowances and credits) (Crespi et al, 2003). Bloom et al (2001) in a study of the effect of fiscal incentives on R&D spending used an econometric model of R&D investment for nine countries from 1979 to 1997 to investigate the relationship between the level of R&D expenditure and tax changes (a ten per cent decrease in the cost of R&D via tax incentives caused a one per cent increase in the short term level of R&D and ten per cent in the longer term). Similar results have been found for US and Canadian studies (Hall and van Reenan, 2000). Furthermore, there is little evidence as to whether non-R&D performing companies can be influenced by tax incentives (Crespi et al, 2003). Governmental considerations over the contribution to R&D are still influenced by supply push and market failure models and the case for market failure is affected by high private and social returns for R&D (Steinmueller, 1994).

Conclusions

It has been recognised that the technological development of small firms is influenced by various sources of know-how including R&D, industry contacts, learning, ICT and publications. R&D is therefore a major source for technological progress in the modern economy. A principal justification for support of R&D policy activities will rest upon the positive spillovers which are the positive externalities from R&D (Revesz and Boldeman, 2006). The studies undertaken in the literature have revealed the major concepts involved in the study of R&D in industrial sectors. In particular the importance of R&D in enhancing technology absorption is considered important for small firms. The approach to the assessment of R&D activity in this chapter has therefore been to focus down from the national (macro) level of policy making to consider the sectoral regional level (meso) and the individual small business level (micro).

Recommended Reading

Acs, Z. and Audretsch, D. (1990) *Innovation and Small Firms*, MIT Press, Cambridge, MA.

References

Acs, Z.J., Audretsch, D.B. and Feldman, M.P. (1994) R&D Spillovers and Innovative Activity, *Managerial and Decision Economics*, 15(2), March, pp. 131-138.

Adams, J.D. (1990) Fundamental Stocks of Knowledge and Productivity Growth, *Journal of Political Economy*, 98(4), pp. 673-703.

Adams, J.D. (1993) Science R&D and Invention Potential Recharge: U.S. Evidence, *American Economic Review*, 83(2), pp. 458-462.

Allen Consulting (2005) *The Economic Impact of Co-operative Research Centres in Australia – Delivering benefits for Australia*, Report for the Co-operative Research Centres Association.

Arrow, K.J. (1962) Economic Welfare and the Allocation of Resources for Invention, *The Rate and Direction of Inventive Activity*, Princeton University, National Bureau of Economic Research.

Arundel, A. (2001) The relative effectiveness of patents and secrecy for appropriation, *Research Policy*, 30, pp. 611-624.

Audretsch, D. (1995) *Innovation and Industry Evolution*, MIT Press, Cambridge, MA.

Audretsch, D.B. and Vivarelli, M. (1996) Firm's Size and R&D Spillovers: Evidence from Italy, Small Business Economics, 8(3), June, pp. 249-258.

Bloom, N. et al (2001) Issues in the design and implementation of an R&D tax credit for UK firms, *IFS Briefing Note*, No. 15, January.

Bönte, W. (2003) R&D and productivity: internal versus external R&D – evidence from West German manufacturing firms, *Economics of Innovation and New Technology*, 12, pp. 343-360.

Bresnahan, T.F. (1986) Measuring the spillovers from technical advance: mainframe computers in financial services, *American Economic Review*, 76(4).

Caballero, R.J. and Jaffe, A.B. (1993) *How high are the giants' shoulders: An empirical assessment of knowledge spillovers and creative destruction in a model of economic growth*, National Bureau of Economic Research, Working Paper No. 4370, Cambridge, Massachusetts.

Coe, D. and Helpman, E. (1995) International R&D Spillovers, *European Economic Review*, 39(5), pp. 859-887.

Cohen, W.M. (1995) Empirical studies of innovative activity, in P.Stoneman (ed.) *Handbook of the Economics of Innovation and Technical Change*, Blackwell, Oxford.

Cohen, W.M. and Levinthal, D.A. (1989) Innovation and learning: the two faces of R&D, *Economic Journal*, 99, pp. 569-596.

Cohen, W.M. and Levinthal, D.A. (1990) Absorptive capacity: a new perspective on learning and innovation, *Administrative Science Quarterly*, 35, pp. 128-153.

Crespi, G., Patel, P. and von Tunzelmann, N. (2003) *Literature Survey on Business Attitudes to R&D*, Science Policy Research Unit (SPRU), Brighton, University of Sussex.

David, P.A., Hall, B.H. and Toole, A.A. (2000) Is public R&D a complement or substitute for private R&D?: a review of the econometric evidence, *Research Policy*, 29, pp. 407-530.

Department of Communications, Information Technology and the Arts (DCITA) (2005) *Productivity Growth in Service Industries*, Occasional Economic Paper, Canberra.

Dodgson, M. and Rothwell, R. (eds.) (1994) *The Handbook of Industrial Innovation*, Edward Elgar, Aldershot.

Eaton, J. and Kortum, S. (1996) Trade in ideas: patenting and productivity in the OECD, *Journal of International Economics*, 40, pp. 251-278.

Eaton, J. and Kortum, S. (1999) International technology diffusion: theory and evidence, *International Economic Review*, 40(3), pp.537-570.

Etzkowitz, H. and Leydesdorff, L. (eds.) (2002) The Triple Helix: special issue of *Research Policy*, 29(2).

Fisher, F.M. and Temin, P. (1973) Returns to scale in research and development: what does the Schumpeterian hypothesis imply? *Journal of Political Economy*, 81, pp. 56-70.

Gittleman, M. and Wolff, E. (1998) R&D activity and cross country growth comparisons, in Archibugi, D. and Michie, J. (eds.), *Trade, Growth and Technical Change*, Cambridge University Press.

Griffith, R., Redding, S. and Reenen van J. (2004) Mapping the two faces of R&D: productivity growth in a panel of OECD Industries, *The Review of Economics and Statistics*, 86(4), pp. 882-895.

Griliches, Z. (1957) Hybrid corn: An exploration in the economics of technological change, *Econometrica*, 25(4).

Grilliches, Z. (1992) The search for R&D spillovers, *The Scandinavian Journal of Economics*, 94, pp. 29-47.

Hall, B. and van Reenan, J. (2000) How effective are fiscal incentives for R&D?: a review of the evidence, *Research Policy*, 29, pp. 449-470.

Hirsch-Kreinsen, H., Jacobson, D. and Robertson, P. (2005) 'Low Tech' Industries: Innovativeness and Development, Perspectives a Summary of a European Research Project, Pilot Project Consortium, Dortmund, Germany.

Jaffe, A. and Tratjenberg, M. (1998) *International knowledge flows: evidence form patent citations*, NBER Working Paper No. 6507, USA.

Jaffe, A.B., Tratjenberg, M. and Henderson, R. (1993) Geographic localisation of knowledge spillovers as evidenced by patent citations, *The Quarterly Journal of Economics*.

Jaruzelski, B., Dehoff, K. and Bordia, R. (2005) The Booz Allen Hamilton global innovation 1000, *Strategy and Business*, 41, Winter.

Kealey, T. (1996) *Economic Laws of Scientific Research*, Macmillan, London.

Kodama, F. (1991) *Analysing Japanese High Technologies*, Pinter, London.

Kohn, M. and Scott, T.J. (1982) Scale economies in research and development, *Journal of Industrial Economics*, 30, pp. 239-250.

Lederman, D. and Maloney, W.F. (2003) *R&D and Development*, World Bank Research Paper 3024.

Levin, R., Klevorick, A.K., Nelson, R. and Winter S.G. (1987) *Appropriating the Returns from Industrial Research and Development*, Brookings Papers on Economic Activity, 3, Washington D.C.

Maddock, R. (2002) Social costs and benefits from public investment in innovation, *Business Council of Australia*, paper No. 2, pp. 88-93.

Mandeville, T.D., Lamberton, D.M. and Bishop, E.J. (1982) *Economic Effects of the Australian patent system*, AGPS, Canberra.

Mansfield, E. (1985) How rapidly does new industrial technology leak out?, *The Journal of Industrial Economics*, 34(2), December.

Mansfield, E., Rapoport, J. Romeo, A, Wagner, S. and Beardsley, G. (1977) Social and private rates of return from industrial innovations, *Quarterly Journal of Economics*, 71, pp. 221-240.

Mansfield, E., Schwartz, M. and Wagner, S. (1981) Imitation Costs and Patents: An Empirical Study, *The Economic Journal*, 91.

Martin, B., von Tunzelmann, N., Ranga, M. and Geuna, A. (2003) *Review of the literature on the size and performance of research units: report for OST*, SPRU, University of Sussex.

Mazzoleni, R. and Nelson, R.R. (1998) The benefits and costs of strong patent protection: a contribution to the current debate, *Research Policy*, 27, pp. 273-284.

Mitchell, G. and Hamilton, W. (1988) Managing R&D as a strategic option, *Research Technology Management*, 31(3), pp. 15-22.

Mohnen, P. (1996) R&D externalities and productivity growth, Science, *Technology and Innovation*, 18, pp. 39-66.

Mowery, D.C. and Rosenberg, N. (1979) The influence of market demand upon innovation: a critical review of some recent empirical studies, *Research Policy*, 8, pp. 103-153.

Myers, S. (1984) Finance theory and finance strategy, *Interfaces*, 14, pp. 126-137.

Nadiri, M.I. and Theofanis, P.M. (1994) The Effects of Public Infrastructure and R&D Capital on the Cost Structure and Performance of U.S. Manufacturing Industries, *Review of Economics and Statistics*, 76(1), February, pp. 22-37.

Nelson, R.R. (1990) Capitalism as an engine of progress, *Research Policy*, 19.

OECD (2002) Tax Incentives for Research and Development, trends and issues, OECD, Paris.

Organisation for Economic Co-operation and Development (OECD) (2002) *Frascati Manual*, OECD Publications, Paris.

Phillips, R. (1997) *Innovation and Firm Performance in Australian manufacturing*, Industry Commission Staff Research paper, AGPS, Canberra.

Polanyi, M. (1943) Patent Reform, *Review of Economic Studies*, 11(1).

Pottelsberghe de la Potterie van, B. and Lichtenberg, F. (2001) Does foreign direct investment transfer technology across borders?, *The Review of Economics and Statistics*, 83(3), pp. 490-497.

Quah, D. (2003) Digital goods and the new economy, in Jones, D.C. (ed.) *New Economy Handbook*, Elsevier Academic Press, USA, pp. 291-323.

Revesz, J. (1999) *Trade-Related Aspects of Intellectual Property Rights*, Staff Research paper, Productivity Commission, Canberra.

Revesz, J. and Boldeman, L. (2006) *The economic impact of ICT R&D: a literature review and some Australian Estimates*, Occasional Economic Paper, Australian Government Department of Communications, Information Technology and the Arts, Commonwealth of Australia, November, pp. 1-140.

Revesz, J. and Lattimore, R. (2001) *Statistical Analysis of the Use and Impact of Government Business Programmes*, Staff Research Paper, Productivity Commission, Canberra.

Robson, M. Townsend, J. and Pavitt, K. (1988) Sectoral patterns of production and use of innovations in the UK: 1945-1983, *Research Policy*, 17, pp. 1-14.

Scherer, F.M. (1982) Inter-industry technology flows in the US, *Research Policy*, 11, pp. 227-246.

Scherer, F.M. and Ross, D. (1990) *Industrial Market Structure and Economic Performance*, Third edition, Houghton-Mifflin, Boston.

Schuchman, H. (1981) Information Transfer in Engineering, The Futures Group, Washington D.C.

Schumpeter, J. (1934) *The Theory of Economic Development*, Harvard University Press, Massachusetts, USA.

Schumpeter, J. (1942) *Capitalism, Socialism and Democracy*, Harper, New York.

Scotchmer, S. (2004) *Innovation and Incentives*, MIT Press, Cambridge, Massachusetts.

Sena, V. (2004) The return of the prince of Denmark: a survey of recent developments in the economics of innovations, *The Economic Journal*, 114, pp. 312-332.

Shanks, S. and Zheng, S. (2006) *Econometric Modelling of R&D and Australia's Productivity*, Productivity Commission Working Paper, April.

Steinmueller, W.E. (1994) Basic research and industrial innovation, in M.Dodgson and R.Rothwell (eds.) *The Handbook of Industrial Innovation*, Edward Elgar, Aldershot, Chapter 5.

Taylor, C.T. and Silbertson, Z.A. (1973) The economic impact of the patent system: A study of the British experience, Cambridge University Press.

Teece, D.J. (1986) Profiting from technological innovation: implications for integration, collaboration, licensing and public policy, *Research Policy*, 15, pp. 285-305.

Tidd, J., Bessant, J. and Pavitt, K. (2001) *Managing Innovation: integrating technological, market and organisational change*, Second edition, Wiley, Chichester.

Trajtenberg, M. (1990) *Economic Analysis of Product Innovation, The Case of CT Scanners*, Harvard Economic Studies, Harvard University Press, Cambridge, Massachusetts.

Von Tunzelmann, G.N. (1995) Technology and Industrial Progress: the foundations of economic growth, Edward Elgar, Aldershot.

Von Tunzelmann, N. (2003) Historical co evolution of technology and governance, *Structural Change and Economic Dynamics*.

Von Tunzelmann, N. (2004) Technology in post war Britain, in R.Floud and P.A.Johnson (eds.) *The Economic History of Britain since 1700*, Third edition, Cambridge University Press, Cambridge.

Von Tunzelmann, N. and Efendioglu, U. (2001) Technology, growth and employment in post war Europe: short-run dynamics and long-run patterns, in P.Petit and L.Soete (eds.) *Technology and the Future of European Employment*, Edward Elgar, Cheltenham, pp. 46-77.

Walker, W. (1980) in K.Pavitt (ed.) *Technical Innovation and British Economic Performance*, Macmillan, London.

4. Technology Diffusion

"For a successful technology, reality must take precedence over public relations, for Nature cannot be fooled."

RICHARD P. FEYNMAN (1918-1988)

This chapter at a glance

- Introduction
- Technology Diffusion
- Technology Transfer Networks
- A Model of Technology Diffusion
- "Best practice"
- Implications for Policy
- Conclusions

Introduction

It is evident that Governments today regard technology diffusion as an important route to increased competitiveness, especially diffusion into small businesses (La Rovere, 1998; Tran and Kocaoglu, 2009) with advantages of flexibility, dynamism and responsiveness. However, small firms have disadvantages related to the lack of technological and financial resources which can lead not only to problems in their ability to source technology but also in their capability to absorb it into their organisation and diffuse it into their industrial sector (Jones-Evans, 1998).

The objectives of this chapter are threefold: first, to investigate technology diffusion (Brooksbank et al, 2001) in the form of new or improved technology through formal and informal networks enabling learning by interacting; second, to develop a model of technology diffusion including external sources, channels of technology transfer, and mechanisms involved in the transfer of technology into the innovative small business; and third, to relate the model to "best practice" and to note situations where "low activity" can be improved. Finally, the implications for policy relevant to technology and entrepreneurship arising from the model of technology diffusion are investigated and conclusions drawn.

Since there is a time dimension involved in the study of the diffusion of technology into small businesses, similar to other investigations of innovation, theories based on these studies will tend to lag behind the "best" current practices. All models of technology diffusion, including refined models such as the Bass Norton model, are a simplification of reality (Islam and Meade, 1997) and, therefore, have a measured influence upon policy. One theoretical model that has informed policies is the Centre Periphery Model (Schon, 1971) which rests on three basic assumptions -

i) the technology to be diffused exists prior to its diffusion,
ii) technology diffusion takes place from the source outwards to small businesses, and
iii) the support of technology diffusion involves incentives, provision of resources and training.

This model is shown in Figure 4.1.

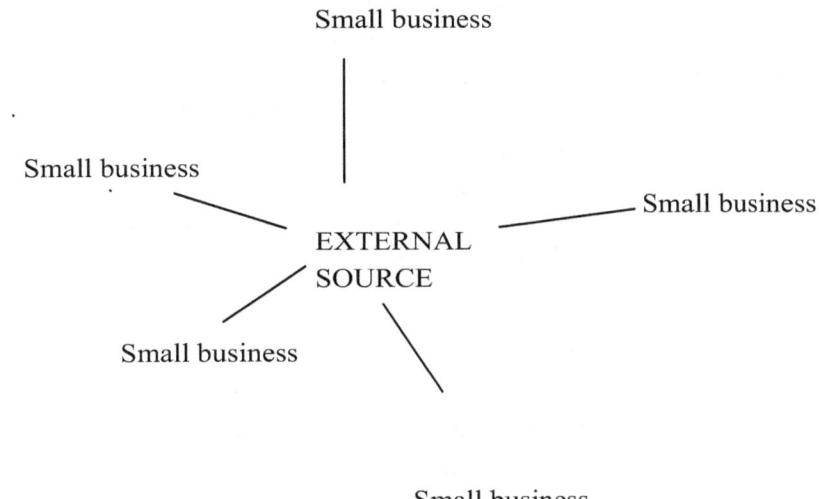

Figure 4.1 Centre-Periphery Model

By applying the Centre-Periphery Model to Technology Transfer Network Theory it is possible to construct what can be described as the "Hub and spoke" or "Star" network. This is a simple construct that can be used as a building block for more intricate networks. Diffusion will take place from the source of the technology through channels by a "diffuser", using a transfer mechanism, to the small firm. The effectiveness of the system will depend upon the resources available to the external source to enable the transfer, the efficiency of the diffuser and the mechanism involved, and the ability of the small company to acquire technology. The scope of the system will vary directly with the level of technology and the flow of information.

Technology Diffusion

When a new technique has been adopted the speed at which other small businesses adopt may differ widely. This leads to what can be called the rate of diffusion (imitation). The rate of diffusion will be faster, the greater the improvement over existing technology and, the lower the cost of the technology in general (Roy and Cross, 1975). Using the definition of Bradley, et al (1995) technology diffusion can be defined as the spread of a new technique from one small firm to another ('inter-firm diffusion') (Stoneman and Karshenas, 1993). The two principal types of technology diffusion are "disembodied" diffusion (the transmission of knowledge and technical expertise) and "embodied" diffusion (the introduction into production processes of machinery, equipment and components incorporating new technology) (Papaconstantinou, Sakurai and Wyckoff, 1995). Research spillovers are the means by which new knowledge or technology developed by one firm become potentially available to others and the absorptive capacity of the receiving firms will determine the extent to which the technology is incorporated.

The time pattern of adoption and the speed at which it takes place are distinct happenings. The exploration time period when implementing an innovation can provide imitators with a "window of opportunity" to proliferate (Jayanthi, 1998). Empirical studies suggest that the adoption of a new technology follows a bell-shaped, or normal, distribution curve (Norris and Vaizey, 1973). By plotting cumulatively this shows the number of small businesses who have adopted a new technology in any given year, and the distribution will give an 'S'- shaped curve. (It was Gabriel Tarde who in the Laws of Imitations, 1903, proposed that adoptions plotted against time assume a normal distribution, or if plotted cumulatively assume the 'S'-shaped curve.) (Baker, 1976; Pijpers et al, 2002; UoT, 2004) An 'S'-shaped distribution, not necessarily derived from a normal distribution, shows the spread of most new technology. There are two general reasons for the occurrence of this distribution.

(i) The diffusion process for small businesses is a learning process.

Small businesses who are potential users have to become aware of the technology and then to attempt to evaluate it. Consequently they may use the technology on a trial basis. The learning process takes place at this stage. Information about the technology has to be disseminated, and as it is adopted by other small firms, or by the small company on an experimental basis the information becomes more reliable. The importance of accumulated knowledge and expertise is an important factor determining whether firms are likely to adopt new technology or to act as sources of innovation (Gurisatti, Soli and Tattara, 1997). 'Bugs' will be overcome, which will in turn reduce the risk of adopting the technology. The concept of the individual small business learning curve can be extended to a network group of small firms where experience with a new technology increases as each successive small company adopts the new technology. As a result, the distribution of small businesses adopting a technology might be expected to yield a normal curve.

(ii) An interaction effect occurs for small businesses.

When only a small number of small businesses have adopted a technology, there are a small number of diffusers who can generate information on the technology and from whom the technological idea can spread. Diffusion rates at this point are low. When the number using the technology increases the "information base" broadens and because there is still a considerable number of small firms who have not adopted the new technology the rate of diffusion increases. When there is a large proportion of small companies using the technology the number of potential small businesses still remaining becomes small. The remaining small firms will be resistant to change and there will be a slow down in the cumulative number of small companies using the new technology. This will yield an 'S'-shaped curve. The first formal study of diffusion was the spread of hybrid corn (Grilliches, 1960). The adoption rate in different states in the USA was studied and it was found that there were significant differences between states in the rate of hybrid corn adoption. Logistic growth curves were fitted by Grilliches to his data and the parameters found from the curves for the different states showed wide variations.

Another formal study of the rate of diffusion was carried out by Mansfield who studied the rate of diffusion of twelve innovations in four industries - coal, iron and steel, brewing and rail (Mansfield, 1961, 1968). Although small firms were not included in the analysis, for medium-sized and large firms in most cases, the spread of innovations over time approximated the 'S'-shaped curve. According to Mansfield the spread of innovations is best described by a logistic curve.

Despite the shape of the curve for technology diffusion appearing `S'-shaped, there will be differences in the speed at which technology is diffused and the length of the diffusion process. Both within and between industries there will be considerable variations in the rate of the diffusion of technology between small businesses.

Important factors which appear to affect the rate of diffusion (speed at which a new technology is accepted) are the characteristics of the small business and the characteristics of the technology itself. Early work on the categories of adopters found that further to adoption following a normal distribution curve the distribution could be used to show the categories of adopters (Rogers, 1962). Table 4.1 shows the categories of adopters with the majority of adopters lying between the mean and the mean minus/plus the standard deviation on the normal distribution curve.

	Table 4.1 The Categories of Adopters				
Categories	Innovators	Early Adopters	Early Majority	Late Majority	Laggards
Number of Adopters	2.5%	13.5%	34%	34%	16%
	x - 2σ	x - σ	x	x + σ	
	Years				

The categories of adopters can be described as follows:

Innovative small businesses are those who want to explore new technologies. They will have relationships with other firms in their network, and with suppliers and customers.

Early adopters will be those who will adopt new technology if it is to their advantage. Since they will act as 'opinion leaders' their influence will be greater than innovative small businesses.

The *early majority* will be intentional while the *late majority* will be sceptical and will adopt when the technology has diffused.

Last, the *laggards* will be so late adopting a new technology that it will have been superseded.

The categories of adopters show that small businesses which adopt an innovation independently are innovators (Tassopoulos and Papachroni, 1998). Early research studies aimed at defining the characteristics of adopters found that early adopters relied to a greater extent on impersonal sources of information from wider and more sources (Rogers, 1962). They used sources in close contact with the origin of new ideas including technical journals. Small firms that are early adopters will tend to be "technically progressive" and will be close to the best that can be achieved in the practice of applying technology (Carter and Williams, 1957). On this assumption a progressive small company will take a wide range of authoritative technical journals, will have a variety of contacts with sources of technology including similar small businesses, and will assess ideas from these sources. It is expected that communication within the small firm will be well organised and co-ordinated and there will be a willingness to share knowledge with other small companies in its network. A progressive small business will set its standards by reference to best practice in other small firms.

The speed of diffusion will also be faster the greater the awareness of small businesses to the advantages of adopting a new technology. The process of communication will be important here as well as the ability of small firms to assess the merits of the technological advance. A small company is more likely to adopt a new technology as it diffuses due to being under increasing competitive pressure to do so, through the technology becoming more attractive, and as a result of information about the technology being broadcast from an increasing base (Green and Morphet, 1975).

Technology Transfer Networks

Technology transfer networks are of particular importance to small businesses with little in-house resources and experience to explore the potential of new technologies. Small firms usually lack awareness to the value of technology transfer, are diffident to enabling services, and therefore rely on co-operation with others. Two basic mechanisms available to small companies are technology exchange (technology passed from one small business to another) and technology exploitation (technology transferred to a small firm from an external source).

Technology transfer networks enable small business to reach a common understanding regarding new technologies quickly. Important aspects of technology transfer networks are the type and size of the network. Whereas, small networks appear more efficient, since communications are easy and network dynamics controllable, large networks benefit from a greater pool of resources. There are four principal types of networks. The "star" network has already been reported. A "nodal linkage" network involves small firms on an equal footing and is not suitable for those businesses with different levels of experience. "Ad hoc" or "informal" networks are those without a formal structure where small companies intimately know each other concentrating communication where required. These tend to be mature networks, but are not well suited for heterogeneous groupings, or those with little commonality between small businesses. "Regional" networks are the most complex type consisting of multi-tiered structures linking local networks. These are suitable for heterogeneous small firms. The descriptions of these four types of network are exemplars in their purist form. Networks adapt to changing internal and external factors and evolve from one (centre-periphery) to another (multi-tiered). Although co-operation with other technology transfer networks provides the possibility of accessing a wider contact base it carries with it some competitive risk.

A Model of Technology Diffusion

A model of the diffusion of technology into small businesses can be described as innovation (supply) from the source of technology (origins) and diffusion (demand) to the small firm (destination). The model can be expressed concisely in algebraic form:

Origins	$i = 1, 2, \ldots m$
Destinations	$j = 1, 2, \ldots n$
Supply at each origin	a_i
Demand at each destination	b_j
Constraint; supply = demand	$\sum a_i = \sum b_j$

In order to find a solution we must specify the variable x_{ij} as the unit(s) of technology transferred from origin i to destination j over time t.

All supply	$\sum_j x_{ij} = a_i$	$j = 1, 2 \ldots n$
All demand	$\sum_i x_{ij} = b_j$	$i = 1, 2 \ldots m$

The diffusion of technology D can be expressed:

$$D = \left[\sum_{i=1}^{m} \sum_{j=1}^{n} \right] x_{ij}$$

where $i = 1, 2, \ldots m$ and $j = 1, 2, \ldots n$

The rate of diffusion of a new technology can be likened to waves of adoption involving distinct time packages. This is illustrated in Table 4.2.

	Table 4.2 The Rate of Diffusion				
	Innovators	Imitators			
Waves of adoption	1st Wave	2nd Wave	3rd Wave	4th Wave	5th Wave
Categories	Innovators	Early Adopters	Early Majority	Late Majority	Laggards
Number of Adopters	2.5%	13.5%	34%	34%	16%
Time Periods	Period 1	Period 2	Period 3	Period 4	Period 5
Diffusion = for each period	$\left[\sum_{i=1}^{m} x_{ij}\right]_1$	$\left[\sum_{j=1}^{n} x_{ij}\right]_2$	$\left[\sum_{j=1}^{n} x_{ij}\right]_3$	$\left[\sum_{j=1}^{n} x_{ij}\right]_4$	$\left[\sum_{j=1}^{n} x_{ij}\right]_5$

The rate of diffusion (R) can be calculated according to time (t) (number of years) as follows:

$$R = \frac{\left[\sum_{i=1}^{m} \sum_{j=1}^{n}\right] x_{ij}}{t}$$

where $i = 1, 2, \ldots m$ and $j = 1, 2, \ldots n$

This equation is a temporal model (Thomas et al, 2001) of technology diffusion which measures the speeds of diffusion (or rates of technology transfer) (Bradley, McErlean, Kirke, 1995).

Technology transfer is an active process whereby technology is carried across the border of two or more social entities (the external source and the small business), and technology transfer channels are the link between the entities (in which various technology transfer mechanisms are activated) (Autio and Laamanen, 1995). A technology transfer mechanism is defined as any specific form of interaction between entities during which technology is transferred (Autio and Laamanen, 1995). The ability to establish external linkages is of critical importance to small firms and a critical mass of small company users will spread the usage and acceptance of the technology (Jain, 1997). The success or uptake of technology depends on how successful the performed community of (implied or ideal) users match the characteristics of actual users (Woolgar, Vaux, Gomes, Ezingeard and Grieve, 1998). Success can be achieved by "configuring the user". Further to this Malecki has stated that "as new technology and products are learned, acquired, evaluated, and improved upon, a firm or region comes to know about best-practice technology ..." (Malecki, 1991, p.122). Laranja calls these "cumulative processes of learning" (Laranja, 1994, p.173).

"Best practice"

Technology transfer networks are one of the best forums for small businesses to learn from each other, to exchange experiences, and to diffuse technology. The typical areas where the benefits of "best practice" can be found are technology transfer skills (determining a small firm's needs by auditing and drawing-up agreements and contracts), technological expertise and know-how (including standards and regulatory issues), service provision (assembling the provision of services), and management and organisation (public relations) (Commission of the European Communities, 1998).

Networks are usually segmented by geographical region, industry sector or by technology and they can work with a mixed sector-technology focus. The danger with specialisation is that it carries the disadvantage that eventually the potential market will be exhausted. It is possible to overcome this by anticipating and looking for opportunities in complementary technology areas.

"Best practice" procedures for the diffusion of technology within networks usually include minimum standards for the small businesses, external funding apportionment, expected performance, and confidentiality. Procedures will usually become less formal over time due to ideal size attainment and growth realisation. Good practice for the successful operation of a network is the realisation by small enterprises that it is not only an alliance of enterprises but also a partnership of entrepreneurs. (Entrepreneurs will act as technological gatekeepers and will have an important role to play in the operation of networks.) (Thomas, 1999) This needs to be reflected in network communications and good relationships between the small firms will form the basis of good practice for the operation of the network.

Success in the diffusion of technology within networks is often the result of small businesses following "best practice" and this usually involves performance management. This is not easy to attain since the process of technology transfer can be long and without success, the results of the network are difficult to define and there may be discrepancies between the small firms. "Low" activity may arise due to conflicts in a network. When these are efficiently managed and resolved they provide opportunities for the small companies to broaden their experience and widen their understanding of other small firms' views. When they are not conflict may lead to "low" activity. Conflict management and identification will form part of the "best practice" of successful technology diffusion. Typical examples of "low" activity are misunderstanding between small companies, different objectives and motives and under-performance of a small business.

Implications for Policy

The implications for policy of a model of the diffusion of technology into small businesses, and the technology processes involved, necessitates the need to formulate technology transfer related action. This includes raising small firms' awareness of the potential of technology transfer to help solve problems and the existence of networks to provide practical support. Once small companies comprehend the possible benefits of technology transfer they will need more help to realise the benefits. Two further types of action to achieve this are specific support provided to individual small businesses (assistance during the establishment of network relationships) and technology transfer support to small firms in general (to foster technological knowledge and establish network links from external sources such as universities and research providers for the dissemination of know-how into small companies).

Coupled to the three forms of policy action described above the three main types of external sources involved in the diffusion of technology to small businesses are public and non-profit organisations (regional and national development organisations (RDOs/NDOs), regional technology advice centres (RTACS) and chambers of commerce), private consultants (technology brokers, management consultants, patent attorneys), and Research and Technology Organisations (RTOs) (contract research firms, science parks and technology centres). Technology transfer networks may comprise all three types although homogeneous networks are usually easier to form and develop. Amongst the three types public bodies are best placed to undertake policy programmes, private companies concentrate on providing focused assistance and RTOs provide technology knowledge and know-how. For small firms involved in technology transfer networks key mechanisms include information transfer (newsletters and databases), technology transfer (R&D audits), skills transfer (training) and specialist support (financial guidance). Value for money of the mechanisms will be a key policy measure. There will need to be care that changes in policy will not make a small company withdraw from technology transfer activities and that policy reacts to difficult situations by providing small businesses with incentives.

Conclusions

Although the variables involved in the model appear to be the most important influences on technology diffusion into small businesses there will also be a multiplicity of influences that accelerate or alleviate the rate of diffusion. This spectrum of influences on diffusion rates broadens when considering technology transfer among the various different small firms in multi-tiered networks. An extension of the hypothetical example of diffusion is the diffusion of technology into small companies through multi-tiered networks. In these sociological forces will have an important role to play. The rate of adoption of a new technology will be faster if it is compatible with the previous experience and present normative values of small businesses. Other influences on the speed of diffusion include the complexity of the new technology and random influences.

The model illustrates that the successful diffusion of a new technology involves considerably more than technical competence. Many complementary factors will be prominent and a small business may be retarded in its acquisition of technology by other small firms who are slow to adopt. `Laggards' can have a deleterious effect on the diffusion of technology by other small companies. The rapid diffusion of a technology will be facilitated by a willingness of small businesses to make adjustments.

Recommended Reading

Thomas, B. (1999) A Model of the Diffusion of Technology into SMEs, Proceedings of the 44th International Council for Small Business (ICSB) World Conference: Innovation and Economic Development, Naples, 20-23 June.

References

Autio, E. and Laamanen, T. (1995) Measurement and evaluation of technology transfer: review of technology transfer mechanisms and indicators", *Int. J. Technology Management*, 10(7/8), pp. 643-664.

Baker, M.J. (1976) Chapter 7, "Diffusion Theory and Marketing", in *Marketing Theory and Practice*, London, Macmillan, pp. 119-131.

Bradley, A., McErlean, S. and Kirke, A. (1995) "Technology Transfer in the Northern Ireland food processing sector", *British Food Journal*, 97(10), pp. 32-35.

Brooksbank, D., Morse, L., Thomas, B. and Miller, C. (2001) Technology Diffusion, *Entrepreneur Wales*, Western Mail.

Carter, C. and Williams, B. (1957) *Industry and Technical Progress*, London, Oxford U.P.

Commission of the European Communities (1998) *Good Practice in Technology Transfer*, DGXIII Telecommunications, Information Market and Exploitation of Research, Luxembourg, EU.

Green, K. and Morphet, C. (1975) Section 7, "The Diffusion of Innovations", in *Research and Technology as Economic Activities*, York, Science in a Social Context (SISCON), pp. 45-47.

Grilliches, Z. (1960) "Hybrid Corn and the economics of innovation", *Science*, 29 July, 275-280.

Gurisatti, P., Soli, V. and Tattara, G. (1997) "Patterns of Diffusion of New Technologies in Small Metal-Working Firms: The Case of an Italian Region", *Industrial and Corporate Change*, 6(2), March, pp. 275-312.

Islam, T. and Meade, N. (1997) "The Diffusion of Successive Generations of a Technology: A More General Model", *Technological Forecasting and Social Change*, 56(1), pp. 49-60.

Jain, R. (1997) "A Diffusion Model for Public Information Systems in Developing Countries", *Journal of Global Information Management*, 15(1), Winter, pp. 4-15.

Jayanthi, S. (1998) "Modelling the Innovation Implementation Process in the Context of High-Technology Manufacturing: An Innovation Diffusion Perspective", Cambridge, ESRC Centre for Business Research.

Jones-Evans, D. (1998) *"SMEs and Technology Transfer Networks - Project Summary"*, Pontypridd, Welsh Enterprise Institute, University of Glamorgan.

La Rovere, R.L. (1998) "Diffusion of information technologies and changes in the telecommunications sector: The Case of Brazilian small- and medium-sized enterprises", *Information Technology and People*, 11(3), pp. 194-206.

Laranja, M. (1994) "How NTBFs Acquire, Accumulate and Transfer Technology: Implications for Catching-Up Policies of Less Developed Countries such as Portugal", in *New Technology-Based Firms in the 1990s*, (ed. by Oakey R.), London, Paul Chapman, pp. 169-180.

Malecki, E.J. (1991) Technology and economic development: the dynamics of local, regional, and national change, New York, Longman.

Mansfield, E. (1961) "Technical change and the rate of imitation", *Econometrica*, October, pp. 741-766.

Mansfield, E. (1968) Chapter 4, "Innovation and the Diffusion of New Techniques", in *The Economics of Technological Change*, New York, Norton, pp. 99-133.

Norris, K. and Vaizey, J. (1973) Chapter 7, "The Diffusion of Innovations", in *The Economics of Research and Technology*, London, George Allen and Unwin, pp. 86-103.

Papaconstantinou, G., Sakurai, N. and Wyckoff, A.W. (1995) "Technology Diffusion, Productivity and Competitiveness: An Empirical Analysis for 10 Countries, Part 1: Technology Diffusion Patterns", Brussels, European Innovation Monitoring System (EIMS).

Pijpers, R.E., Montfort, van, K. and Heemstra, F.J. (2002) Acceptable van ICT: Theorie en een veldonderzoek onder top managers, *Bedrijfskunde*, 74(4).

Rogers, E. (1962) *Diffusion of Innovations*, New York, Collier-Macmillan.

Roy, R. and Cross, N. (1975) Section 3.1.3, "Diffusion", in *Technology and Society*, T262 2-3, Milton Keynes, The Open University Press, pp. 36-38.

Schon, D.A. (1971) Chapter 4, "Diffusion of Innovation", in *Beyond the Stable State*, London, Temple Smith, pp. 80-115.

Stoneman, P. and Karshenas, M. (1993) "The diffusion of new technology: extensions to theory and evidence", in *New Technologies and the Firm: Innovation and Competition* (ed. By Swann P.), London, Routledge, pp. 177-200.

Tassopoulos, A. and Papachroni, M. (1998) Penetration models of new technologies in Greek small and medium-sized enterprises, *Int. J. Technology Management*, 15(6/7), pp. 710-720.

Thomas, B. (1999) "The Role of Technological Gatekeepers in the Management of Innovation in SMEs: The Regional Context", *COrEx*, 12 March.

Thomas, B., Packham, G. and Miller, C. (2001) A Temporal Model of Technology Diffusion into Small Firms in Wales, *Industry and Higher Education*, August.

Tran, T.A. and Kocaoglu, D.F. (2009) Literature review on technology transfer from government laboratories to industry, *Management of Engineering and Technology*, August, pp. 2771-2782.

University of Twente (UoT) (2004) Diffusion of Innovations Theory, *Theorieenoverzicht* TCW, http://www.utwente.nl/cw/theorieeboverzicht.

Woolgar, S., Vaux, J., Gomes, P., Ezingeard, J.-N. and Grieve R. (1998) "Abilities and competencies required, particularly by small firms, to identify and acquire new technology", *Technovation*, 18(8/9), pp. 575-584.

5. Clusters and Knowledge Flows

"All men are caught in an inescapable network of mutuality."

MARTIN LUTHER KING (1929-1968)

This chapter at a glance:

- Introduction
- Clusters and Knowledge Flows
- Mobility within clusters
- Example of the Inkjet Printing Cluster in the Cambridge area
- Conclusions

Introduction

According to Oliver and Porta (2006) sticky knowledge (Lagendijk, 2000, p. 165) or knowledge accumulations (Florida, 2002; Storper and Venables, 2002) constitute the available intellectual capital (IC) sources of a cluster. Sticky knowledge is described as the knowledge embedded in the local industrial milieu which is difficult to copy or transfer to other areas (Oliver and Porta, 2006). Furthermore, sharing knowledge involves firms with a community of workers in a cluster (Harrison, 1991). IC arises from knowledge creation through linkages between firms (knowledge spillovers), firms and institutions, and informal relationships arising from an interaction process in a local skilled labour pool. Knowledge in the cluster is tacit, embedded and transferred within the cluster (Oliver and Porta, 2006).

Three mechanisms for the transfer of knowledge within a cluster identified by Keeble and Wilkinson (1999) include new firms, spin-offs from firms, universities and public sector research laboratories, interactions between the makers and users of capital equipment, interactions between customers and suppliers, and inter-firm mobility of the labour in the cluster. The relationships and mechanisms create flows within the cluster and the knowledge transfer processes result in cumulative know-how that is external to firms remaining internal to the cluster (Oliver and Porta, 2006). Empirical evidence has shown how knowledge sustainability (expenditure on education), regional economic outputs (earnings and labour productivity), knowledge capital (patents and R&D) and human capital (high tech employment) components have influenced regional competitiveness (Porter, 1990). Economic productive activities are enabled by tacit knowledge, the contribution of local businesses and infrastructures such as research institutes and universities, by employee exchange and the mobilisation of human capital resources (Oliver and Porta, 2006). According to the resource-based view of the firm (Penrose, 1959; Peteraf, 1993) the competitive advantage of companies arises from the core competences or knowledge of firms.

An important element of a cluster is the community of people (Harrison, 1991). Indeed, Porter's (1990) model included the skilled labour pool involving territorial human resources specialisation in clusters. Representing a cluster resource, the skilled labour pool is available to cluster firms (people educated on specific cluster university courses and trained through educational programmes in cluster requirements) (Oliver and Porta, 2006). In addition to training and education there are the social capital aspects associated with tacit knowledge and information flows attributable to directors, managers and workers in cluster companies (Uzzi, 1996). It has been reported by Dahl and Pedersen (2004) that in clusters knowledge flows take place through informal contacts. The local labour pool will contain the available pool of entrepreneurship, competences, education and traditional crafts (Oliver and Porta, 2006). But absorptive capacity is needed to capture, use and disseminate knowledge within the cluster (Zahra and George, 2002).

This chapter investigates the movement of labour in the Cambridge Inkjet Printing (IJP) cluster. Labour mobility and knowledge spillovers in clusters are interrelated phenomena with knowledge embodied in entrepreneurs and specialised workers spilling over from one enterprise to another through labour mobility and direct revelation (Guarino and Tedeschi, 2006). The case study of the movement of labour between the population of IJP companies in Cambridge is described. The mobility rate of labour in the IJP cluster is considered with reference to the growth of the cluster. Through the study of the mobility of labour the value of intellectual capital (IC) in the cluster can be considered (Oliver and Porta, 2006).

Clusters and Knowledge Flows

When investigating how embedded knowledge flows through labour mobility in regional clusters in Denmark Dahl (2002, p. 3) defined a cluster as "a geographically concentrated group of firms active in similar or closely connected technologies and industries with a degree of both horizontal and vertical linkages". He goes on to note that firms are inter-connected through the formation of a local labour market and that this is for a particular kind of labour. Furthermore, with regard to knowledge clusters and the specialisation of technological and economic activities resulting from agglomeration economies, the local labour force is specialised (Marshall, 1890; Piore and Sable, 1984; Krugman 1991(a); (b), Arthur, 1994, Saxenian, 1994; Porter 1998). In the area of the market suited to the companies in the cluster the growth of the cluster creates an increased demand for labour (Dahl, 2002). Feldman (2000) notes that job moves by workers between companies in an industry is influenced by ideas that are embedded in individuals' minds. Such moves allow the accumulated knowledge of the workers during their careers with companies to be taken advantage of by employers. As a result knowledge flows through the movement of workers between companies, and when start ups offer jobs (Dahl, 2002).

When start ups have accumulated experiences from parent companies, this allows knowledge diffusion which has been shown to be important in a number of industries (Franco and Filson, 2000; Klepper, 2002). Reasons why workers move within a cluster include existing social ties and risk aversion (Breschi and Lissoni, 2001). Similar companies in a cluster offer workers wider employment prospects and companies will pay higher salaries for needed knowledge from a previous employee of a similar company. The social and institutional context is important (Breshi and Lissoni, 2001). Employee mobility needs to be supported by the innovation culture involving not only the company but the community (Angel, 1991). Knowledge flows between companies will be greater where the culture and institutional setting of the cluster promote mobility (Dahl, 2002).

To climb the occupational ladder through job mobility requires a change of employer. Hall and Kasten (1976) show that for most job changes there is a move to a higher occupational category involving higher pay. The work of Saxenian (1990; 1994) includes many examples of mobility and inter-firm knowledge flows. But there is only indirect evidence on the link between employee mobility and knowledge flows from the literature (Rosenkopf and Almeida, 2001). One of the first empirical studies to delve further into knowledge spillovers was Zucker and Darby (1996) who found that workers had the skills and knowledge for technological development through the embodiment of ideas. In biotechnology case studies the star scientists (who had made major breakthroughs) drew on their intellectual capital in the innovation process. The knowledge on breakthrough techniques was held by these scientists.

Zucker, Darby and Brewer (1998) found clear linkages between the start-up of biotech firms and star scientists. Further investigation of these aspects was undertaken by Alemeida and Kogut (1997) who used patent data to track the inter-firm moves of the star engineering scientists to trace knowledge and idea diffusion in the semiconductor industry and showed that inter firm mobility enabled the transfer of ideas between companies with subsequent new patents through the star scientists. Franco and Filson (2000) focused on the mobility of employees creating spin offs which diffused knowledge. Patent citation analysis of the semiconductor industry was used by Rosenkopf and Almeida (2001) to study the way in which the search for new knowledge in companies through mobility and alliances was undertaken. They found clear evidence that companies used mobility to fill holes in knowledge (Rosenkopf and Almeida, 2001) which clearly supports inter firm mobility of workers facilitating inter company knowledge flow.

Dahl (2002) reported that in the latter period of cluster development there was entry by multinational firms. Lorenzen and Mahnke (2002) found acquisition of small firms by multinationals resulting in the local business environment changing. It was also found that social networking was discouraged by multinationals which focused on inter company networks (Lorenzen and Mahnke, 2002). This resulted in knowledge diffusion through networks and co-operation decreasing and knowledge diffusion through worker movement subsiding (Dahl, 2002).

It has been noted by Dahl (2002) that there can be mobile and non mobile engineers. It was found that mobile engineers were paid more for their acquisition of knowledge and in job learning than non mobile employees. New companies paid them more than they earned at previous companies because of the knowledge they brought. It has also been found that there is a positive impact of education since a longer education increases the ability to learn and absorb knowledge (Dahl, 2002). Furthermore, mobility appears to have a positive effect on earnings growth. Whether an employee has a degree, masters or PhD affects annual earnings (Dahl, 2002).

Mobility within clusters

In a cluster the mobility of highly qualified labour is an important vehicle for knowledge flow and indicators of the movement that takes place can help the investigation of important linkages. Mobility indicators can be used to determine the effects of the movement of labour on the development of the cluster. A parameter that can be used as an indicator of the potential in a knowledge based cluster is the stock of knowledge and the rate of mobility of labour can be used to indicate innovation potential. Information investigated includes gender, age, education and employment at a particular time and can be used to compare the stock of labour with different types of education across a cluster and describe the flow of labour between companies within the cluster. Higher education institutions (HEIs) and research institutes play an important role in the education and development of the workforce within a cluster. The mobility of highly educated labour is probably the most apparent mechanism of knowledge transfer. Mobility may take place without knowledge transfer and similarly knowledge transfer can take place without the mobility of labour. For example, information and communication technology (ICT) enables knowledge transfer without the physical movement of labour. In addition to the mobility of labour other knowledge transfer mechanisms include buyer-supplier relationships, co-operations, networks, R&D collaborations, staff placements and temporary staff exchange. Further indicators are the number of co-operations and external contacts, joint patents and citations and co-authorships. There is particular interest in the importance of senior labour as a vehicle for knowledge transfer. It has been found that PhD mobility appears to be a weak knowledge transfer mechanism (Stenberg et al, 1996).

A basic assumption is that the mobility of senior labour between companies indicates knowledge transfer. This depends on the ability and opportunity of the labour to learn from the company in which they are employed and on their education and time in employment which are variables that are available for analysis. Also, the occupation and position of senior labour within an organisation influences their learning. Mobility can be considered to be a change of workplace, organisation or company. Knowledge exists in a number of forms including codified knowledge, competencies, formal knowledge, skills and tacit knowledge. The indicator that has been taken to denote the level of knowledge has been formal education. Formal education has advantages over indicators of other forms of knowledge which have data that are difficult to collect and collate. Although the highest level of formal education achieved has limitations as a knowledge indicator it is the most appropriate available. Senior staff will tend to be highly educated (including those with research degrees) with a high degree of specialisation. Here indicators of formal knowledge should be an acceptable knowledge indicator.

The mobility of senior staff will involve both permanent employment and the temporary exchange of labour. There will also be higher and lower mobility exhibited by companies involving both 'movers' and 'stayers' (Graversen et al, 2002). Mobility will arise due to takeovers and acquisitions and it will also result from the entry and exit of companies into a cluster and where firms go out of business or are restructured they will change their identity. This impacts on the definition of mobility in terms of what is 'real' mobility and what is 'artificial' or 'false' mobility caused by change of company ownership in the cluster. As well as change in employment as a focus for knowledge transfer, involving labour transferring knowledge from their previous to their current workplace, there is also the turnover of labour in firms arising from employees leaving and retiring resulting in the employment of new staff from other companies, the unemployed or recent graduates. These employees will contribute to the renewal and flow of knowledge through new knowledge being brought into the company.

With formal education the senior labour's field will be of interest due to potential innovation power - this assumes that labour with high education have a higher level of innovative knowledge than those with intermediate or low education levels. The exchange of labour not only brings new knowledge into companies but also results in the loss of knowledge and the right balance is a major challenge for human resource departments in companies.

'Job to job' mobility involves 'in flows' and 'out flows' for companies. Those workers who have accumulated experience for one company may be viewed as valuable labour for another and will be considered to be experienced workers. If they change employers frequently they can be considered to be 'experienced nomads' (Graversen et al, 2002). On the other hand, inexperienced workers who have a tendency to move are 'inexperienced nomads' and will be recently educated seeking appropriate employment (Graversen et al, 2002). The loss of experienced workers will be considered to be more serious than the loss of those recently employed. Furthermore, senior labour that stays with the same employer will be considered to be stable workers. It has been found that the share of stable workers increases with age and the share of mobile workers decreases with age (Graversen et al, 2002).

Example of the Inkjet Printing Cluster in the Cambridge area

Ink jet printing in the Cambridge area has undergone a period of rapid change in recent years. A shift from a production to a knowledge based cluster has been influenced by acquisitions (Garnsey et al, 2009). In 2001 there were seven industrial inkjet printing companies operating in the Cambridge area: Domino, Inca, Linx, Videojet (who acquired Cambridge based IJP firm ElmJet in 1993), Willett (with headquarters in Corby but with a base in Cambridge), Xaar and Xennia (Garnsey et al, 2010). By mid June 2005 only three of these companies (Domino, Xaar and Xennia) had not been acquired. The Danaher Corporation had created their product identification division through the takeovers of Videojet (2002), Willett (2003) and Linx (2005), and Dainippon Screen Manufacturing Company bought out Inca in June 2005. In 2008 Xaar was taken over by Ten Cate from the Netherlands, leaving only two substantial independent players in the Cambridge ink jet industry: Domino and Xennia. Examples of small businesses operating in the IJP cluster included one of the early firms Biodot with four employees founded in 1994, Xennia with 30 employees founded in 1996, and a later company Inski founded in 2004 (Garnsey et al, 2010).
Firm proximity is largely historical and grounded in the way they have spun out from one another. The transfer of tacit knowledge can be a major benefit of proximity and this is where the main benefits for the Cambridge inkjet firms are realised. The people, skills and knowledge base provided are a significant benefit of being located near to other inkjet printing firms in the Cambridge region. The Cambridge address and the prestige associated may be a significant factor. These are benefits from geographical proximity to other ink jet printing companies but also from being located in the Cambridge high-tech cluster.

The endowment represented by the University of Cambridge provided the critical conditions for the pre-history of the inkjet printing industry, via the creation of Cambridge Consultants Ltd (CCL) by two of its students. Both agglomeration economies and spin-offs have played important roles in the clustering as the firms in the IJP industry that spun-off from CCL moved beyond the orbit of the University. Through international demand for high tech products and services which the inkjet printing companies developed the competence to supply exogenous factors were at work (Stam et al, 2009). Clustering emerged as a self-reinforcing process stimulated by knowledge generation and transfer. It is with labour market advantages and the emergence of specialist suppliers that agglomeration economies are primarily associated. The amplification effects of the spin-off process in the Cambridge IJP industry are apparent in its multi-generational dimension. Here spin-off firms become the source of further spin-offs and attraction of entrepreneurs and firms from outside the region.

Takeover activity in the continuous ink jet printing dominated firms led to the departure of entire organisational operations from the Cambridge area. Departure impacts are still being experienced and there could be further problems for the cluster through negative impacts on the supplier network, reduced personnel movements, the area's reputation and attraction of business and personnel. On the other hand, as a result of redundancies the availability of highly skilled labour could lead to new spinout activity.

There is uncertainty regarding the future of the Cambridge inkjet printing cluster since the industry has undergone significant change resulting from acquisitions, the resultant rationalisation and restructuring, and increased competition from laser and drop on demand. Although many manufacturing operations have moved from the area it is likely that Cambridge will continue as a centre for R&D due to the skills base and the Inkjet Research Centre located at the University of Cambridge Institute for Manufacturing (IfM).

In association with, and supported by, the consortium, the IfM research centre intends to develop understanding of the fundamental behaviour of liquids in environments presented in inkjet printing. The aim of the project is to reduce duplicated research in local companies and to spread the financial burden. This represents the reconnection of the IJP cluster to the Engineering department at the University of Cambridge from which it originated several decades earlier. This should help the cluster to be sustained into the future and to add cohesion and build a reputation.

Conclusions

The example of the IJP case study shows that a local production network exists around companies. An extensive knowledge network has been built around the firms facilitated by senior staff movement between them. Competition within the group is intense and formal collaboration rare, and international concerns and relationships are of importance resulting in well developed global production facilities, suppliers, customers, partners and competitors, and contradictions exist between perceptions of members and the reality of linkages within the cluster. The cluster is local to the region but part of a wider international industry cluster with simultaneous importance of local cluster effects and extensive international links. In the early days of the industrial inkjet printing industry, most firms were associated with a particular technology, but as the industry has matured all of the major players have employed a range of technologies in their products. As a consequence of maturity the focus has shifted from technical development to marketing and distribution of the product.

Further Reading

Garnsey, E., Stam, E. and Thomas, B. (2010) The emergence and development of the Cambridge ink jet printing industry, in Fornahl, D., Henn, S. and Menzel, M-P. (eds.) *Chapter 11, Emerging Clusters: Theoretical, Empirical and Political Perspectives on the Initial Stage of Cluster Evolution*, Cheltenham: Edward Elgar, pp. 265-291.

References

Almeida, P. and Kogut, B. (1997) The Exploration of Technological Diversity and the Geographic Localization of Innovation, *Small Business Economics*, 9, pp. 21-31.

Angel, D.P. (1991) High Technology Agglomeration and the Labour Market: The Case of Silicon Valley, *Environment Planning*, 23, pp. 1501-1516.

Arthur, W.B. (1994) *Increasing Returns and Path Dependence in the Economy*, University of Michigan Press, Stanford.

Breschi, S. and Lissoni, F. (2001) Knowledge Spillovers and Local Innovation Systems: A Critical Survey, *Industrial and Corporate Change*, 19(4), pp. 975-1005.

Dahl, M.S. (2002) Embedded Knowledge Flows through Labour Mobility in Regional Clusters in Denmark, Paper presented at the *DRIUD Summer Conference on "Industrial Dynamics of the New and Old Economy – who is embracing whom?"*, Copenhagen/Elsinore 6-8 June.

Dahl, M.S. and Pedersen, C.O.R. (2004) Knowledge flows through informal contacts in industrial clusters: myth or reality? *Research Policy*, 33, pp. 1637-1686.

Feldman, M.P. (2000) Location and Innovation: The New Economic Georgraphy of Innovation, Spillovers and Agglomeration, in Clark, G.L., Feldman, M.P. and Gertler, M.S. (eds.) *The Oxford Handbook of Economic Geography*, Oxford University Press, Oxford.

Florida, R. (2002) *The Rise of the Creative Class*, Basic Books, New York, NY.

Franco, A.M. and Filson, D. (2000) Knowledge Diffusion through Employee Mobility, Research Department staff Report, No. 272, Federal Reserve Bank of Minneapolis, Minneapolis.

Garnsey, E., Thomas, B. and Stam, E. (2009) *The Emergence and Development of the Cambridge Ink Jet Printing Industry*, Centre for Technology Management Working Paper, No. 2009/4, Institute for Manufacturing, University of Cambridge, 1-30.

Graversen, E.K., Nas, S.O., Ekeland, A., Bugge, M.M., Svanfeldt, C. and Akerblom, M., *Knowledge transfer by labour mobility in the Nordic countries*, Working Paper 2002/1, The Danish Institute for Studies in Research and Research Policy, Aahus, Denmark.

Guarino, A. and Tedeschi, P. (2006) *Endogenous Knowledge Spillovers and Labour Mobility in Industrial Clusters*, Department of Economics and ELSE, University College, London.

Hall, R. and Karsten, R. (1976) Occupational Mobility and the Distribution of Occupational Success Among Young Men, *American Economic Review*, 66(2), pp. 309-315.

Harrison, B. (1991) Industrial districts: old wine in new bottles? *Regional Studies*, 26, pp. 469-483.

Keeble, D. and Wilkinson, F. (1999) Collective learning and knowledge development in the evolution of regional clusters of high technology SMEs in Europe, *Regional Studies*, 33, pp. 295-303.

Klepper, S. (2002) The Evolution of the U.S. Automobile Industry and Detroit as its Capital, paper presented at the *DRUID Winter Conference*, 17-19 January, Rebild, Aalborg, Denmark.

Krugman, P. (1991a) *Geography and Trade*, MIT Press, Cambridge, Massachusetts.

Krugman, P. (1991b) Increasing Returns and Economic Geography, *Journal of Political Economy*, 99(3), pp. 483-499.

Lagendijk, A. (2000) Learning in non-core regions: towards intelligent clusters. Addressing business and regional needs, in Boekema, F., Morgan, K., Bakkers, S. and Rutten, R. (eds.) Knowledge, *Innovation and Economic Growth: The Theory and Practice of Learning Regions*, Edward Elgar, Cheltenham, pp. 165-191.

Lindgren, U. and Eriksson, R. (2007) Cluster Mobility – Impacts of Inter-Firm Labour Mobility on Firm Performance, Paper presented at the *Regional Studies Association International Conference: Regions in Focus?*, Lisbon, Portugal, 2-5 April.

Lorenzen, M. and Mahnke, V. (2002) Global strategy and the acquisition of local knowledge: how MNCs enter regional knowledge systems, Copenhagen Business School, Copenhagen.

Marshall, A. (1890) *Principles of Economics*, Macmillan, London.

Oliver, J.L.H. and Porta, J.I.D. (2006) How to measure IC in clusters: empirical evidence, *Journal of Intellectual Capital*, 7(3), pp. 354-380.

Penrose, E. (1959) *The Theory of Growth of the Firm*, John Wiley & Sons, New York, NY.

Peteraf, M. (1993) The cornerstones of competitive advantage: a resource-based view, *Strategic Management Journal*, 14, pp. 179-191.

Piore, M. and Sabel, C. (1984) *The Second Industrial Divide*, Basic Books, New York.

Porter, M.E. (1990) *The Competitive Advantage of Nations*, The Free Press, New York, NY.

Porter, M.E. (1998) *On Competition*, Harvard Business School Press, Boston.

Rosenkopf, L. and Almeida, P. (2001) *Overcoming Local Search through Alliances and Mobility*, University of Pennsylvania and Georgetown University, Georgetown, Pennsylvania.

Saxenian, A. (1990) Regional Networks and the Resurgence of Silicon Valley, California *Management Review*, 33(1), pp. 39-112.

Saxenian, A. (1994) Regional Advantage: Culture and Competition in Silicon Valley and Route 128, Harvard University Press, Cambridge, MA.

Stam, E., Garnsey, E. and Thomas, B. (2009) Competence creation in the Cambridge Inkjet Printing Industry, *25th EGOS Colloquium, Passion for creativity and innovation*, ESADE Business School, Barcelona, July 2-4, 166.

Stenberg, L., Gustafsson, E. and Marklund, G. (1996) Use of human resource data for analysis of the structure and dynamics of the Swedish innovation system, *Research Evaluation*, 6(2), pp. 121-132.

Storper, M. and Venables, F. (2002) Buzz: the economic force of the city, paper presented at the *Druid Summer Conference*, Copenhagen, 6-8 June.

Uzzi, B. (1996) The sources and consequences of embeddedness for the economic performance of organizations, *American Sociological Review*, 61, pp. 974-998.

Zahra, L.G. and George, G. (2002) Absortive capacity: a review, re-conceptualization and extension, *Academy of Management Review*, 27, pp. 185-203.

Zucker, L.G. and Darby, M.R. (1996) Star Scientists and Institutional Transformation: Patterns of Invention and Innovation in the Formation of the Biotechnology Industry, *Proceedings of the National Academy of Science of the United States of America*, 93, Nov. 12, pp. 709-716.

Zucker, L.G., Darby, M.R. and Brewer, M.B. (1998) Intellectual Human Capital and the Birth of U.S. Biotechnology Enterprises, *American Economic Review*, 88(1), pp. 290-306.

6. Higher Education Spin-offs

"The higher education so much needed today is not given in the school, is not to be bought in the market place, but it has to be wrought out in each one of us for himself ..."

WILLIAM OSLER (1849-1919)

This chapter at a glance:

- Introduction
- Academic Entrepreneurs
- Academic spin-offs
- Economic importance of academic spin-offs
- Conclusions

Introduction

The last twenty years has witnessed a growing enthusiasm for entrepreneurs as catalysts for economic development and change, with increasing attention paid to the role of small technology-based companies as contributors to wealth creation, technological innovation and employment in high technology industries (Autio, 1997; Jones-Evans and Klofsten, 1997; Jones-Evans and Westhead, 1996; Shane, 2004). As a result, there has been considerable academic and policy interest in examining the process of entrepreneurship within such organisations, commonly known as "technical entrepreneurship".

Early studies into technical entrepreneurship identified the research-based academic environment – universities, non-profit research institutes and government research centres - as the predominant background from which technical entrepreneurs emerged (Schrage, 1965; Roberts and Wainer, 1966; Wainer and Rubin, 1969; Cooper, 1971). These individuals would form new businesses which have commonly become known as spin-offs (Carayannis et al. 1998).

However, spin-offs from universities are not a recent phenomenon (Nicolaou and Birley, 2003a&b). Historically, higher education spin-off enterprises can be traced to the 19th century when companies were set-up by academic researchers. Examples of these are the German chemist Heinrich Caro who contributed to the setting up of BASF, and two other academics taught by his master, von Liebig, who helped set-up Hoescht. In the nineteenth and twentieth centuries, many technical academics set up enterprises which have become large multinationals (Mustar, 1995; Mustar et al, 2006) including Werner von Siemens, Gerard Philips and Conrad Schlumberger.

The growth of Silicon Valley can be partly attributed to researchers who left academic and industrial laboratories. For example, William Schockley who was head of the research team at Bell Telephone set up a small company in Palo Alto in 1952 (Zagnoli, 1990), whilst Professor Frederick Terman convinced two of his students, Hewlett and Packard, to set up a new enterprise. In order to start producing an audio-oscillator designed by Hewlett, when writing his masters thesis, Terman lent them $538 which provided them their first employment and also a loan from a bank in Palo Alto.

Academic spinoffs have played a major role in the development of specific industries (Müller, 2008; Druilhe and Garnsey, 2004). The growth of the biotechnology industry is linked directly to the development of small enterprises set up by academic researchers who transferred basic research activities into innovations (Dodgson, 1993). During the 1970s, the biotechnology industry influenced universities to give more attention to control over intellectual property by their researchers and professors (Kennedy, 1986). Financing institutions, especially venture capital companies, became interested in academic research, and this led to a shift in the boundaries between non-commercial basic research and commercial research (Mansfield, 1991, 1995). As suggested by Rosenberg and Nelson (1994), commercialisation was possible, since funding in the biomedical field had created a reservoir of knowledge from which the biotechnology industry developed new products.

During the 1970s, participation by universities in commercialising biotechnology research not only led to new knowledge but also academics starting their own enterprises by maintaining or leaving their academic tenure. As a consequence, spin-off enterprises play a central role in the growth of new industrial sectors and the innovation process.

Academic entrepreneurs

The academics who form spin-off businesses have commonly become known as academic entrepreneurs (Knight, 1988; Klofsten *et al*, 1988; Samson and Gurdon, 1993; Jones-Evans, 1995; Meyer, 2003). They tend to be scientists whose primary occupation, prior to playing a role in the spin-off, and possibly concurrent with that process, was that of clinician, researcher or teacher, affiliated with a university, research institution and/or hospital. They do not include the industrial scientist who, during his/her industrial affiliation, had usually been exposed to corporate and managerial cultures.

This type of technical entrepreneur tend to have little exposure to either the business world or entrepreneurship. However, as Jones-Evans (1995) has recognised that, with the changing nature of academic careers, such individuals could, despite spending the majority of their career in an academic research position, have minor experience of a commercial organisational background, usually within a research department.

Previous research has recognised that the vast majority of the owner-managers of academic spin-offs have considerable technological competence (Mueller, 2006; Druilhe and Garnsey, 2004), from which the product or process which the business bases its competitive advantage is derived. However, there has also been considerable discussion regarding the often highly academic nature of the technological skill and creativity within this type of entrepreneur, leading to some scepticism regarding their ability to manage a commercial enterprise.

Many of the early studies found that technical entrepreneurs rarely possessed management expertise comparable to their technical skills (Cooper, 1971; Schrage, 1965) which was generally attributed to a lack of a formal business education, coupled with work experience which tended to be in the technical area.

More recent studies, such as Westhead and Storey (1994), have also found that the owner-managers of young technology-based firms had limited experience of specific functions such as marketing, finance and personnel. This orthodox view of technical entrepreneurs - having low management experience and high technological expertise - was originally associated with those emerging from a research-based academic environment (Schrage, 1965; Roberts and Wainer, 1966; Wainer and Rubin, 1969).

Studies of academic-based technical entrepreneurs frequently demonstrated that they had very little exposure to management skills and had very little concept of business (Klofsten *et al*, 1988; Samsom and Gurdon, 1990). Detailed research by Jones-Evans (1996a; 1996b) has supported this position, demonstrating that academic entrepreneurs had very little experience of management functions such as marketing or finance, even in the case of those with previous commercial positions.

Whilst academic entrepreneurs have little experience of formal management functions, many will gain 'soft' management skills such as team management and interpersonal skills. This is because academic entrepreneurs have had considerable experience of managing research and development projects, in many cases evolving from a purely technical role within academic research projects, to responsibility for other individuals working together as a team. The inter-personal skills developed during the supervision of small research teams may, in many cases, be directly transferable into the management of a small research-based new venture.

Whilst the lack of management skills and experience may not be a problem at start-up, this may change as the new venture develops. In the extreme case, this may lead to problems if the company grows to the stage where the management responsibilities increase to the point where strong leadership and delegation are needed, but the academic entrepreneurs no longer have sufficient management skills to run the business (Firnstahl, 1986; Greiner, 1972).

These problems could include the delegation of technical tasks to other employees (despite having the capability to do them quicker and better than the employee); shifting from the role of specialist to generalist; watching others achieving a technical competence within the organisation superior to one's own; and learning the new job of general manager (including the tasks of strategic planning, and human resource management).

This may prove very difficult to academic entrepreneurs who possess high technological expertise (Druilhe and Garnsey, 2004). Subsequently, if an entrepreneur with little management experience continues to lead the venture beyond the start-up phase, then the organisational performance of the company will suffer (Flamholtz, 1986). For example, research carried out by Rubenson and Gupta (1990) indicated that founders with scientific or engineering backgrounds remain in control of the companies they founded for shorter periods than do founders whose previous experience was in business.

As well as management skills, the high technological expertise of the individual academic entrepreneur may also lead to considerable problems as the business develops. The dependence of the business on academic entrepreneurs for its technological competence (on which the competitive advantage of the business is often based) can lead to significant problems as the small technology-based firm develops.

Whilst the academic entrepreneur can continue to be involved in product development whilst retaining control as managing director (Maidique, 1980), considerable difficulties may arise in maintaining technological advantage, as often the technical entrepreneur may be the only person within the organisation with the necessary skills and experience to make the relevant technical decisions. In many cases, delegation may be difficult for individuals possessing a high degree of technical expertise, not only because they fear reduced technical quality, but because they have a genuine desire to continue to be involved on the technology side of the business.

In a study of the transition from scientists to managers, Peck (1986) suggested that, for the business to succeed, the entrepreneur's relationship with the product must change from direct to indirect involvement, with a sharp departure from the "hands-on" orientation of the typical scientist. Such a change in roles may be difficult for entrepreneurs whose backgrounds are predominantly technological, despite indications that the future success of the small technology-based firm may rely on the ability of the entrepreneur to tie together the two strands of technical and management experience and expertise (Klofsten and Jones-Evan, 1996; Utterback *et al* 1988; Oakey, 1984).

Academic spin-offs

Academic spin-offs (Müller, 2008; Druilhe and Garnsey, 2004) have their roots in university research through at least one of the founders working in an academic research establishment before inception of a firm (Jones-Evans et al., 1998). These enterprises are established to commercialise a product or service developed in a university laboratory. An academic spin-off usually occurs when a new enterprise is formed by university scientists seeking to develop further the commercial possibilities of their research (Garvin, 1983).

In one of the first studies of small technology-based businesses, Schrage (1965) saw spin-offs as the establishment of a new venture by scientists emerging from their organisation, "Three physicists leave their position with a large corporation or leading university to establish their own company. They pool their funds, secure a research contract from the government, obtain a loan from a friendly bank, and a so-called R&D company is born.". Subsequent studies (Cooper, 1970, 1971; Roberts and Wainer, 1966, 1968; Litvak and Maule, 1971, 1972; Braden, 1977) related 'technical entrepreneurship' directly to founding ventures through spin-offs from university departments (Roberts, 1968; Lamont, 1972; Doutriaux, 1987; Samsom and Gurdon, 1990) or larger organisations (Cooper, 1971, Draheim, 1972).

However, defining academic spin-offs can be difficult. Most studies have related the development of academic spin-offs to two main criteria. First of all, the business must be related to technology developed at the university and secondly, the founder must be a former employee or student of the university who has worked on developing that technology. For example, Cooper (1971) defined high technology spin-off firms as those that have their roots in a research organisation i.e. at least one of the founders worked in a research establishment before starting the firm and was established to commercialise a product developed in a research organisation.

Olofsson and Wahlbin (1984) defined a university technology start-up firm as having at least one founder employed at the university when the company was formed and a business idea which is aimed at commercialising knowledge and technology developed at the university. Other Swedish researchers (McQueen, 1990; McQueen and Wallmark 1988) have referred to a spin-off firm as based on a product or service resulting from university research, and founded (or co-founded) by a person (or persons) from a university research group where the founder moved directly from the university to the spin-off firm (McQueen and Wallmark, 1985;1991). This definition has been adopted for this chapter.

However, this can leave a number of successful companies unaccounted for. For example, does the definition include academics who wish to form a partnership with non academics? For example, Van Tilburg (1990), in a study of spin-offs from the University of Twente, defined a university spin-off as university staff, students and alumni that start their own business, using the university know-how, as well as including individuals from outside the university, who start their own business with assistance and know-how from the University of Twente.

One must also consider the actual involvement of the academic in the business. In a study of academic entrepreneurship in Canadian universities, Doutriaux and Peterman (1982), indicated that all the full professors who started their own business were still employed by the university on either a full-time or part-time basis. Brown (1984) in a study of spin-offs from the University of Utah, showed that the faculty members' participation in a company varied from resigning an academic position and devoting full-time to the company, to following a passive role such as serving as a consultant and/or director of the company. Between these faculty members arranged part-time university appointments and spent the balance of their time with the company.

A wider definitional approach by Giannisis et al. (1991) considers three types of academic spin-off models which are based on the origins of the business itself. The first – the entrepreneurial model – is a newly start-up established as a result of a combination of the expertise and independent motivation that the entrepreneurial faculty member has brought to the commercialisation process. The second type - the traditional model – is where the commercialisation of a university-based technology is pursued by an outside business entity. Finally – the institutional model – is where the commercialisation process is managed by the university through an organisation such as the Industrial Liaison Office (ILO) or a wholly owned not-for-profit subsidiary of the university.

Therefore, whilst a definition may seem easy, in practice there are difficulties in formulating a common definition of an academic spin-off.

Economic importance of academic spin-offs

As we have demonstrated, various studies have recognised that a significant number of new technology-based businesses in both the USA (O'Shea et al, 2005) and Western Europe had been established by scientists emerging from different types of academic-based organisations, such as non-profit research institutes, government research centres and universities. However, despite the increasing interest in the development of spin-offs from academic research, there are only a few studies which have attempted to consider the economic impact of such organisations.

In the USA, a variety of studies have demonstrated how various regions have developed university spin-offs (Saxenian, 1994; Roberts, 1991) although these have tended to concentrate on Route 128 in Boston and Silicon Valley in California as the main examples for spin-off developments from universities such as MIT and Stanford. However, as Malecki (1991) points out, the presence of an outstanding university within a region in the USA does not necessarily lead to the development of an entrepreneurial climate in which high technology spin-offs are created. For example, universities such as Harvard, Columbia, Chicago, Berkeley and Caltech do not play a strong incubator role for such businesses.

In Europe, there are only a few studies which have examined this phenomenon, and only in limited regional settings. Linkoping - one of the fastest growing regions of Sweden - contains a strong high technology industrial environment, which includes the presence of Saab's Aircraft Division, Ericsson Radio and the Swedish Defence Research Establishment, and is at the forefront in the creation and development of new technology-based firms in Sweden. Academics and students from Linkoping University have played a leading role in this. To date, over 450 small technology-based spin-offs have emerged directly from academic research activities at the institution (Klofsten and Jones-Evans, 1996), with a high number of the others using or developing university research findings as the basis for their products or services.

A French study by Mustar (1988, 1995) reported that, from the early 1980s, several hundred French researchers developed high technology enterprises (biotechnology, artificial intelligence and robotics). In an analysis of more than two hundred enterprises, founded by researchers, about one third of all new high technology enterprises were created by public sector researchers. More importantly, academic spin-off enterprises generated three times more employment than other industry and service sectors over the same period. In addition, the failure rate for this type of enterprise was about twenty five percent in the first five years, less than the fifty percent average in the rest of French services and industry.

Italian work on academic spin-off enterprises has been undertaken by Piccaluga (1991; 1992), Amendola (1992) and Bellini and Zolla (1997). The studies found spin-off enterprises to be relatively scarce in Italy although there was growing involvement of universities in entrepreneurial development activities. Amendola (1992) reported that the factor that most influenced the formation of spin-off companies was the quality and status of the academic researcher. According to Chiesa and Piccaluga (1998) it appears that Italian academic status contributes to influencing researchers to choose "soft" entrepreneurial solutions, instead of abandonment of university research centres - a more popular option in other academic systems, especially in America.

In the UK, the most famous study of academic spin-off activity is that of the 'Cambridge Phenomenon', which found that nearly all of the 350 high technology businesses in the area had ultimately been generated from Cambridge University, especially the departments of physics, engineering and computing (Segal, 1986; Segal Quince, 1995, 2000). Similar clusters have been identified at the universities of Heriot Watt and Aston, although these have not been developed to the same extent, and the research on successful spin-outs is quite sparse.

Despite this, the increased recognition of the potential of spin-off businesses to the economy, both in terms of diffusion of university knowledge and high skill employment opportunities, led to a positive policy decision by the UK Government, in 1999, to create more start-ups on campuses (Di Gregorio and Shane, 2003) through the establishment of a £50M University Challenge competition. The programme aimed at establishing venture (seed) capital funds and management support for potential start-ups in the winning universities. These policy aims of the UK Government have been taken on-board by the Higher Education Funding Council for England (HEFCE) and also by the Higher Education Funding Council for Wales (HEFCW) and the Scottish Funding Council.

In Wales, the articulation of policy has been through initiatives such as TOPSPIN and the Wales Spinout programme, although it needs to be recognised that since Wales has a low proportion of companies per head of the population (Wales has 7.51 firms with more than five employees per 1,000 population while England has a figure of 9.60 per 1,000 population) the emphasis on spin-off activity will need to relate to this difference. In Scotland, as enunciated in a report by Scottish Enterprise (1996) and a study by Downes and Eadie (1997; 1998), the Scottish case is different again. Following analysis of twenty five companies, the report maintained that universities were involved in all cases. This shows that the recognition of the importance of spin-offs took place at an earlier time in Scotland than in many other parts of the UK.

In order to encourage more university-based staff with innovative ideas and "know-how" to start their own businesses, the UK Government also provided £25M for eight new enterprise centres in universities (particularly in science and engineering areas). This included a reach-out fund of £20M a year to reward universities for strategies and activities that enhanced interaction with business and promoted technology transfer.

Whether these approaches are the right way to develop entrepreneurial businesses is still open to debate. The role of universities in creating these milieux of innovative firms (Elco van Burg et al, 2008) within different regions has led to a proactive approach by universities, usually supported by regional or national government, in adopting direct entrepreneurial roles. However, these can range from the establishment of university-owned holding companies to the promotion of fledgling academic entrepreneurs (Gibson and Smilor, 1991) to the development of specific centres of research and training which promote and assist the process of spin-off of academic research into a network of industrial firms and business ventures (Klofsten and Jones-Evans, 1996).

Although there is no recommended model for the creation of spin-off businesses on UK university campuses, there are individual university models and this has resulted in the establishment of a variety of commercial infrastructures on campuses, often alongside the development of incubators and science/technology parks.

In the Netherlands, the Twente regional economy was almost destroyed in the 1960s with the demise of its textile industry, and the loss of fifty thousand jobs. The Technical University, established about this time, had by the late 1970s implemented a spin-off policy for graduates and others to form their own technology-based companies in the area. The scheme, formalised as the TOP programme in 1983, has since then supported the creation of more than one thousand five hundred quality jobs, developing a dynamic young firm community forming the centre of self-sustaining regional regeneration. Following this, the Twente team guided the UNISPIN Innovation Programme's project, for other EU regions to develop similar schemes (Innovation and Technology Transfer, 1997).

Brett et al. (1991) and Roberts (1991) describe the American case which appears to be more dynamic and structured than in Europe, due to the different institutional nature of universities in America. Here there are several environments in which spin-off enterprises can be set up (including incubators and science parks). Universities are also good at commercialising research. For example, the Bank of Boston reported that MIT spin-off enterprises contributed around ten billion dollars a year and three hundred thousand jobs to the Massachusetts economy.

Conclusions

Perhaps one of the real barriers to the development of university spin-off businesses is the culture within the university sector towards entrepreneurship. Whilst the UK government's programmes are aimed at breaking this down and making involvement with industry easier, the traditional academic culture does not encourage the development of links with small-scale industry.

As Louis et al (1989) suggest, universities are not traditionally viewed as leaders in entrepreneurship. In fact, they suggest that there is often a tendency to distinguish between the search for truth in science - which is considered a legitimate function of the university - and the search for invention - which is considered an inappropriate focus on ideas that have potential commercial or practical applicability via spin-off activity. Indeed, it has been indicated that many academics are concerned that research collaboration with industry is against the central ethics of universities, which should focus on fundamental research and the education of students, and that links with industry not only detract from this but could, in some cases, restrict the free flow of information between academics and institutions (Charles and Howells, 1992).

In addition, another problem may be the role of suitable role models for academics to follow (Stankiewicz, 1986; 1994). Most academics are driven to becoming teachers and scholars and therefore tend to perceive other roles with scepticism and even open hostility. As a result, an academic who aspires to become an entrepreneur finds himself in an environment where he is regarded as an oddity. This is an issue which universities need to seriously address through making the 'third role' – interaction with industry – as important as teaching or research.

Recommended Reading

Thomas, B., Packham, G., Miller, C. and Brooksbank, D. (2004) An Appraisal of the SEED University Technology Small Firms Project in Industrial South Wales, *International Journal of Entrepreneurship Education*, 2(3), pp. 307-328.

References

Amendola, G. (1992), L'imprenditorialita difficile: la creazione in Italia di imprese high-tech de parte di ricercatori universitari in Matinelli F., Bartolomei G. (a cura di), Universita e Tecnopoli, Tacchi, Pisa.

Autio, E. (1997) New technology-based firms in innovation networks. In D. Jones-Evans and M. Klofsten (eds.) *Technology, Innovation and Enterprise - The European Experience*, London: MacMillan, pp. 209-235.

Bellini, E. and Zollo, G. (1997) University-industry relationship: empirical evidences on academic spin-off in Southern Italy. Paper presented at the *II International Workshop on Innovation, SMFs and local development*, Cremona, Italy, June 11-12, 1997.

Braden, P.L. (1977) Technological entrepreneurship - the allocation of time and money in technology based firms, *Michigan Business Reports*, No 62, University of Michigan.

Brett, A.M., Gibson, D.G. and Smilor, R.W. (eds.) (1991) *University Spin-off Companies*, Rowman & Littlefield Publishers.

Brown, W.S. (1984) A proposed mechanism for commercialising university technology, In Hornaday, J.A., Tarpley, F., Timmons, J.A. and Vesper, K.H. (eds.), *Frontiers of Entrepreneurship Research*, Babson College, Wellesley, MA, pp. 136-158.

Carayannis, E.G., Rogers E.M. Kurihara, K., Allbritton, M.M. (1998) High-technology spin-offs from government R&D laboratories and research universities, *Technovation*, 18(1), pp. 1-11.

Charles, D. and Howells, J. (1992) *Technology transfer in Europe: public and private networks*, London: Belhaven Press.

Chiesa, V. and Piccaluga, A. (1998) Transforming rather than Transferring Scientific and Technological Knowledge - The Contribution of Academic 'Spin Out' Companies: The Italian Way in Oakey, R. and During, W. (eds.) *New Technology-based Firms in the 1990s*, Volume V, Paul Chapman, London.

Cooper, A.C. (1970) The Palo Alto Experience, *Industrial Research*, (May), pp. 58-60.

Cooper, A.C. (1971) *The Founding of Technologically-based Firms*, Milwaukee, Wisconsin: Centre for Venture Management.

Di Gregorio, D. and Shane, S. (2003) Why Do Some Universities Generate More Start-Ups than Others? *Research Policy*, 32(2), pp. 209-227.

Dodgson, M. (1993) *Technological Collaboration in Industry*, Routledge, London.

Doutriaux, J. (1987) Growth pattern of academic entrepreneurial firms, *Journal of Business Venturing*, 2, pp. 285-297.

Doutriaux, J. and Peterman, B.F. (1982) Technology transfer and Academic Entrepreneurship, In Vesper, K.A. (ed.) *Frontiers of Entrepreneurship Research*, Babson College, Wellesley, MA, pp. 430-448.

Downes, R. and Eadie, G. (1997) The creation and support of academic 'spin out' companies, Paper presented at the *High-Technology Small Firms Conference*, Manchester, 29-30 May.

Downes, R. and Eadie, G. (1998) The Creation and Support of Academic Spin-Out Companies, In Oakey, R. and During, W. (eds.) *New Technology-Based Firms in the 1990s*, Volume V, Chapter 2, pp. 4-14.

Draheim, K.P. (1972) Factors influencing the rate of formation of technical companies, in Cooper, A.C. and Komives, J.L. (eds.) *Technical Entrepreneurship: a symposium*, Milwaukee Centre for Venture Management, pp. 3-27.

Druilhe, C. and Garnsey, E. (2004) Do Academic Spin-Outs Differ and Does it Matter? *The Journal of Technology Transfer*, 29, pp. 269-285.

Elco van Burg, A., Romme, G.L., Gilsing, V.A. and Reymen, I.M.M.J. (2008) Creating University Spin-Offs: A Science-Based Design Perspective, Journal of Production *Innovation Management*, 25, pp. 114-128.

Firnstahl, T.W. (1986) Letting go, *Harvard Business Review,* 64(5), pp.14-16.

Flamholtz, E.G. (1990), Growing pains: How to manage the transition from an entrepreneurship to a professionally managed firm, Jossey-Bass Publishers, Oxford.

Garvin, D.A. (1983) Spin-offs and the new firm formation process, *California Management Review*, 25(2), pp. 3-20.

Giannisis, D., Willis, R.A. and Maher, N.B. (1991) Technology commercialisation in Illinois, In Brett, A.M., Gibson, D.V. and Smilor, R.W. (eds.), *University spin-off companies - economic development, faculty entrepreneurs and technology transfer*, Rowman and Littlefield Publishers, Savage, Maryland, pp. 197-221.

Gibson, D.V. and Smilor, R.W. (1991) "The role of the research university in creating and sustaining the US Technopolis." In Brett, A.M., Gibson, D.V. and Smilor, R.W. (eds.), *University spin-off companies - economic development, faculty entrepreneurs and technology transfer*, Rowman and Littlefield Publishers, Savage, Maryland, pp. 31-70.

Greiner, L.E. (1972) Evolution and revolution as organisations grow, *Harvard Business Review*, 50(4), pp. 37-46.

Jones-Evans, D. (1995) A typology of technology-based entrepreneurs: a model based on previous occupational background, *International Journal of Entrepreneurial Behaviour and Research*, 1(1), pp. 26-47

Jones-Evans, D. (1996a) Experience and entrepreneurship - technology-based owner-managers in the UK, *New Technology Work and Employment,* 11(1), pp.39-54.

Jones-Evans, D. (1996b) Technical entrepreneurship, strategy and experience, *International Small Business Journal*, 14(3), pp. 15-40.

Jones-Evans, D. (1995) Definition of Academic Spin-offs - A Discussion Paper, *PHARE-ACE Workshop meeting, Academic Entrepreneurship in Central and Eastern Europe*, Aston Business School, Birmingham, December 14th-15th.

Jones-Evans, D. and Klofsten, M. (1997) Universities and local economic development - the case of Linköping, Sweden, *European Planning Studies*, 5(1), pp. 77-94.

Jones-Evans, D. and Westhead, P. (1996) High technology small firm sector in the UK, *International Journal of Entrepreneurial Behaviour and Research,* 2(1), pp. 15-35.

Jones-Evans, D., Steward, F., Balazs, K. and Todorov, K. (1998) Public Sector Entrepreneurship in Central and Eastern Europe: a study of academic spin-offs in Bulgaria and Hungary, *Journal of Applied Management Studies*, 7(1).

Kennedy, D. (1986), Basic research in the universities: how much utility? In Landaur, R. and Rosenberg, N. (eds.) *The Positive Sum Strategy*, National Academy Press, Washington DC.

Klofsten, M., Lindell, P., Olofsson, C. and Wahlbin, C. (1988), "Internal and external resources in technology-based spin-offs". In Kirchoff, B.A., Long, W.A., McMullan, W.E., Vesper K.H. and Wetzel, W.E.(eds), *Frontiers of Entrepreneurship Research*, Babson College, Wellesley, MA, pp. 430-443.

Klofsten, M. and Jones-Evans, D. (1996) Stimulation of Technology-Based Small Firms - A Case Study Of University-Industry Co-operation, *Technovation*, 16(4), pp. 187-193.

Klofsten, M., Jones-Evans, D. and Lindell, P. (1997) *Growth factors in technology-based spin-offs: A Swedish study*, Piccola Impresa, 1, pp13-38.

Knight, R.M. (1988), "Spin-off entrepreneurs : how corporations really create entrepreneurs". In Kirchoff, B.A., Long, W.A., McMullan, W.E., Vesper K.H. and Wetzel, W.E.(eds), *Frontiers of Entrepreneurship Research*, Babson College, Wellesley, MA, pp. 134-149.

Lamont, L.M. (1972) Entrepreneurship, technology and the university, *R&D Management*, 2(3), pp. 119-123.

Litvak, I.A. and Maule, C.J. (1971) *Canadian Entrepreneurship: a study of small newly established firms*, University Grant Program Research Report Dept. of Industry, Trade and Commerce, Ottowa, Canada.

Litvak, I.A. and Maule, C.J. (1972) Managing the entrepreneurial enterprise, *Business Quarterly*, 37(2), p. 43.

Louis, K.S., Blumenthal, D., Gluck, M.E. and Stoto, M.A. (1989) Entrepreneurs in Academe - an exploration of behaviours among life scientists, *Administrative Science Quarterly*, 34, pp. 110-131.

Maidique, M.A. (1980) Entrepreneurs, champions and technological innovation, *Sloan Management Review,* 21(2), pp. 59.

Malecki, E.J. (1991) *Technology and regional development,* Harlow, Longman.

Mansfield, E. (1991) Academic research and industrial innovation, *Research Policy*, 20, pp. 1-12.

Mansfield, E. (1995) Academic research underlying industrial innovations: sources, characteristics, and financing, *The Review of Economics and Statistics*.

McQueen, D.H. (1990) Entrepreneurship in technical universities: a comparison between ETHZ, Zurich, Switzerland and CTH, Goteborg, Sweden, In Birley, S. (ed.) *Building European Ventures*, Elsevier, Amsterdam, pp. 86-103.

McQueen, D.H. and Wallmark, J.T. (1985) Support for new ventures at Chalmers Univrsity of Technology, In Hornaday, J.A., Shiels, E.B., Timmons, J.A. and Vesper, K.H. (eds.) *Frontiers of Entrepreneurship Research*, Babson College, Wellesley, MA, pp. 609-620.

McQueen, D.H. and Wallmark, J.T. (1988) Growth patterns in technical innovations, In Birley, S. (ed.) *European Entrepreneurship - Emerging Growth Companies*, EFER, Amsterdam, pp. 132-158.

McQueen, D.H. and Wallmark, J.T. (1991) University technical innovation: spin-offs and patents in Goteborg, Sweden, In Brett, A.M., Gibson, D.V. and Smilor, R.W. (eds.), *University spin-off companies - economic development, faculty entrepreneurs and technology transfer*, Rowman and Littlefield Publishers, Savage, Maryland, pp. 103-115.

Meyer, M. (2003) Academic Entrepreneurs or Entrepreneurial Academics? Research based Ventures and Public Support Mechanisms, *R&D Management*, 33(3), pp. 107-115.

Mueller, B. (2006) *Human capital and successful academic spin-off*, ZEW Discussion Papers, 06-81.

Müller, K. (2008) *Academic Spin-Off's Transfer Speed – Analyzing the Time from Leaving University to Venture*, Danish Research Unit for Industrial Dynamics, Druid Working Paper, No. 08-07, pp. 1-28.

Mustar, P. (1988) Science and innovation, Annuaire raisonne de la creation d'enterprises technoliques par les chercheurs en France, Economics, Paris.

Mustar, P. (1995), The creation of enterprises by researchers: conditions for growth and the role of public authorities in OECD (eds.) *High-Level workshop on SMEs: employment, innovation and growth*, Washington DC, 16-17 June.

Mustar, P., Renault, M., Colombo, M.G., Piva, E., Fontes, M. and Lockett, A. (2006) Conceptualising the Heterogeneity of Research-Based Spin-offs: A Multi-dimensional Taxonomy, *Research Policy*, 35(2), pp. 289-308.

Nicolaou, N. and Birley, S. (2003a) Academic Networks in a Trichotomous Categorisation of University Spinouts, *Journal of Business Venturing*, 18(3), pp. 333-359.

Nicolaou, N. and Birley, S. (2003b) Social Networks in Organizational Emergence: The University Spinout Phenomenon, *Management Science*, 49(12), pp. 1702-1725.

Oakey, R.P. (1984) *High Technology Small Firms*, Pinter, London.

Olofsson, C. and Wahlbin, C. (1984) Technology-based new ventures from technical universities: a Swedish case, In Hornaday, J.A., Tarpley, F., Timmons, J.A. and Vesper, K.H. (eds.), *Frontiers of Entrepreneurship Research*, Babson College, Wellesley, MA, pp. 192-211.

O'Shea, R., Allen, T.J., Chevalier, A. and Roche, F. (2005) Entrepreneurial Orientation, Technology Transfer and Spinoff Performance of U.S. Universities, *Research Policy*, 34(7), pp. 994-1009.

Peck, W.F. (1986) The Leadership Transition from Scientist to Manager, *First International Conference on Engineering Management*, Arlington, Virginia, Sept 22nd-24th.

Piccaluga, A. (1991) Gli spin-off accademici nei settori ad alsta tecnologia. Il cao dell'area pisana, Sinergie, 25-26 maggio-dicembre.

Piccaluga, A. (1992) From profs to profits: how Italian academics generate high technology ventures, *Creativity and Innovation Management*, 1, 2, June.

Roberts, E.B. (1968) Entrepreneurship and technology: a basic study of innovators, *Research Management*, 11, pp. 249-266.

Roberts, E.B. (1991) *Entrepreneurs in High Technology*, Oxford University Press, New York.

Roberts, E.B. and Wainer, H.A. (1966) *Some characteristics of technological entrepreneurs, Sloan School of Management*, MIT, Cambridge, Massachusetts, Working Paper, No. 195-6.

Roberts, E.B. and Wainer, H.A. (1968) New Enterprises on Route 128, *Science Journal*, 412, pp. 78-83.

Rosenberg, N. and Nelson, R. (1994) American universities and technical advance in industry, *Research Policy*, 23.

Rubenson, G.C. and Gupta, A.K. (1990), "The Founder's Disease : a critical re-examination". In Churchill, N.C., Bygrave, W.D., Hornaday, J.A., Myzuka, D.F., Vesper, K.H. and Wetzel, W.E. (eds.) *Frontiers Of Entrepreneurship Research,* Babson College, Wellesley, Massachusetts, pp. 167-183.

Samson, K.J. and Gurdon, M.A. (1990) Entrepreneurial scientists: Organisational performance in scientist started high technology firms, Paper presented at the *Frontiers of Entrepreneurship Research Conference*, Babson Centre for Entrepreneurial Studies, Wellesley, Massachusetts.

Samson, K.J. and Gurdon, M.A. (1993), University scientists as entrepreneurs - a special case of technology transfer and high tech venturing, *Technovation,* 13(2), pp. 63-71.

Saxenian, A. (1994) Regional Advantage – Culture and competition in Silicon valley and Route 128, Boston: Harvard.

Schrage, H. (1965) The R&D entrepreneur: profile of success, *Harvard Business Review*, 43(6), pp. 8-21.

Scottish Enterprise (1996) *Science and Technology: Prosperity for Scotland*, Commercialisation Enquiry, Preliminary Research Report, Glasgow.

Segal, N. (1986), "Universities and technological entrepreneurship in Britain - some applications from the Cambridge Phenomenon", *Technovation*, 4, pp. 189-204.

Segal Quince & Partners (1985) The Cambridge Phenomenon: The Growth of High Technology industry in a University Town, Cambridge: SQ&P.

Segal Quince & Partners (2000) The Cambridge Phenomenon Revisited – a synopsis of the new report by Segal Quince Wicksteed, Cambridge: SQ&P.

Shane, S. (2004) Academic Entrepreneurship: University Spinoffs and Wealth Creation, Cheltenham, UK: Edward Elgar.

Stankiewicz, R. (1986) Academics and Entrepreneurs: Developing University-Industry Relations, Frances Pinter Publishers, London.

Stankiewicz, R. (1994) Spin-off companies from universities, *Science and Public Policy*, 21(2).

Utterback, J.M., Meyer, M., Roberts, E., and Reitberger, G. (1988) Technology and industrial innovation in Sweden: a study of technology-based firms formed between 1965 and 1980, *Research Policy*, 17(1), pp. 15-26.

Van Tilburg, J.J. (1990) Dutch high tech spin-off creation, Paper presented at the *20th Anniversary European Small Business Seminar*, Dublin, Ireland, 11th - 14th September.

Wainer, H.A. and Rubin, I.M. (1969) Motivation of Research and Development Entrepreneurs :determinants of company success, *Journal of Applied Psychology*, 53(3), pp. 178-184.

Westhead, P. and Storey, D. (1994) An assessment of firms located on and off science parks in the United Kingdom, HMSO, London.

Zagnoli, P. (1990) I rapporti tra imprese nei settori ad alat tecnoligia. Il cao della Silicon Valley, Giappichelli, Torino.

7. Global Start-ups and business development

"The whole of the global economy is based on supplying the cravings of two per cent of the world's population."

BILL BRYSON (1946-)

This chapter at a glance:

- Introduction
- Characteristics of Global Start-ups
- Global Start-ups: Case Studies
- Conclusions

Introduction

Rialp-Criado et al (2002) noted several key driving forces behind the emergence of global start-ups as well as their age, industry affiliation, export behaviour and performance, geographic distribution, (rise in) number and size. In addition, international operations from the start-up of the business have been seen to be important. General consensus has provided that the underlying notion and theoretical definition of the global start-up phenomenon perceives them as young entrepreneurial firms engaged in international business from inception (Rialp-Criado et al, 2002). On the one hand, researchers have considered a six-year period as the standard in measuring international operations from the start-up of the business (Oviatt and McDougall, 1997). On the other hand, academics have selected other criteria to empirically define the global start-ups being analysed. Rennie (1993) has reported that firms began exporting two years after foundation on average and realised seventy-six per cent of their total sales by exporting. Other authors have defined this according to foreign sales of twenty-five per cent or more after starting exporting activities and within three years of birth (Knight & Cavusgil, 1996; Madsen et al, 2000; Servais & Rasmussen, 2000).

By describing, understanding and interpreting the reasons behind the emergence of global start-ups it is possible to gain insight into their needs for business support provision. Interestingly, according to Rialp-Criado et al (2002), much of the present literature about global start-ups has been assumed to be concerned with high tech businesses, considering the globalisation aspects present in sectors within which these firms compete (Bell, 1995; Coviello & Munro, 1995; Roberts & Senturia, 2000; McDougall & Oviatt, 1996; Burgel & Murray, 2000, Autio & Sapienza, 2000; Autio et al, 2000; Zahira et al, 2000).

Characteristics of Global Start-ups

According to Rialp-Criado et al (2002), the top ten characteristics considered as critical success factors (CSFs) for global start-ups (not in rank order) are:

- "managerial global vision from inception
- high degree of previous international experience on behalf of managers
- management commitment
- strong use of personal and business networks (networking)
- market knowledge and market commitment
- unique intangible assets based on knowledge management
- high value creation through product differentiation, leading edge technology products, technological innovativeness (usually associated with a greater use of IT), and quality leadership
- niche focussed, proactive international strategy in geographically spread lead markets around the World from the very beginning
- narrowly defined customer groups with strong customer orientation and close customer relationships
- flexibility to adapt to rapidly changing external conditions and circumstances" (Rialp-Criado et al, 2002, pp. 25-26).

Further to this, Rialp-Criado et al (2002) from their research into twenty seven of the most important studies in the decade 1993-2002, which consider global start-ups amongst other forms of these types of businesses, say that having identified, examined and critically assessed these studies they have been able to formulate an adequate observation of the state of the art of this important research area within the field of International Entrepreneurship (IE).

According to Wakkee et al (2003), global start-ups are described in the literature as perfect examples of entrepreneurial ventures and therefore need to be investigated from an entrepreneurial perspective. They go on to say that, the concept of global start-up was first mentioned in a paper by Mamis (1989). At about the same time, Ray (1989) undertook four cases for which the term global start-up was used. Following this, the term global start-up was defined by Oviatt and McDougall (1994) "as one that seeks to derive significant competitive advantage from extensive co-ordination along multiple organisational activities, the location of which is geographically unlimited" (pp. 59-60). Wakkee et al (2003) add that, these firms do not only respond to global market conditions, they also act to acquire resources and sell wherever in the World there is the largest value.

Since Oviatt and McDougall (1994, 1995) the term global start-up has been little used. A number of authors, including Harveston (2000), Madsen and Servais (1997) and Saarenketo (2002), have also referred to global start-ups. More recently Rasmussen and Madsen (2002) have suggested that they are the only type of international new venture. Wakkee et al (2003) have said that "a global start-up is the most radical manifestation of the international new venture because it derives significant competitive advantage from extensive co-ordination along multiple organisational activities, the location of which is geographically unlimited. Such firms not only respond to globalising market conditions but they also proactively pursue opportunities to acquire resources and sell outputs, wherever in the world they have the greatest value" (pp. 6-7). According to Wakkee et al (2003), from their discussion of the literature on the definition of a global start-up, five relevant characteristics are apparent, and these are:

"(1) the diversity or scope of the international activities

(2) the company age

(3) the timing of international activities (time to entry)

(4) the global diversity of the international activities

(5) the purpose of the international activities (strategic choice)" (Wakkee et al, 2003, p. 13).

In fact, they say that the nature of the opportunity differences global start-ups from other types of start-ups since the opportunity is a global one. From this Wakkee et al (2003) define a global start-up as:
"A new venture that from its inception ("opportunity recognition") seeks to pursue opportunities wherever they arise (i.e. global or in an unlimited number of countries around the world), it co-ordinates multiple activities in the value chain through the interaction with network actors around the World. The entrepreneur(ial team) leading the firm is internationally experienced and skilled." (Wakkee et al, 2003, p. 14).

They go on to say that global start-ups are characterised by high levels of entrepreneurial orientation (EO) although originally developed by Lumpkin and Dess (1996) and Lumpkin (1998) for established firms when considered for global start-ups they exhibit high levels of EO. In these terms Wakkee et al (2003), bring together the descriptions of global start-ups and, describe them as "an entrepreneurial firm that literally from its inception is involved in a variety of international activities around the World" (Wakkee et al, 2003, p. 28).

The case studies selected in this chapter are spin-offs, from a "new" university, which are believed to have global potential and exhibit differing states of technological innovativeness. Those that have been selected are university spin-offs operating in the global market or with a global potential. Founders, closely involved with the spin-offs from establishment until now, have been interviewed. No restrictions have been placed with regard to the spin-off age and industry. Although, it is the case that spin-offs running for a number of years will provide more valuable information about their development than those only recently founded. For spin-offs in existence for many years it may be difficult to find a founder who has been involved with the business since the original idea. It might also be more difficult for these people to remember the specific problems encountered in the early stages of the development of the spin-off. Spinout managers identified the interesting spin-off cases and provided contact names for interviews. They also approached the companies in the first instance to gain their support. The stages of development of the case study companies have also been measured.

Global Start-ups: Case Studies

Described below are the six global start-up case studies, which were investigated, and these reveal different characteristics and aspects for business development. Perhaps the main limitation is that most of the companies are in the early stage of business development, but it is envisaged that this work will be developed into a longitudinal study which will show interesting evolutionary dynamics in future years. Due to the sensitive nature and stage of their development all the companies have been referred to anonymously.

Consultancy Services

The Consultancy Services (CS) company, founded in January 2004 as a University spinout, commenced trading in January 2005 to assist organisations access European Union (EU) funding in order to implement specific projects in accordance with regulations accompanying the use of funds. In particular the Internet has been used to interact with organisations who, as the customers, need to access EU funds. This has been taken into account in the company's overall marketing strategy and e-business strategy. Services involve a range of training courses that cover all aspects of European Union (EU) funded projects, including State Aid Rules and Public Procurement Directive. CS has a team of Prince 2 practitioners and freelance consultants. Table 7.1 summarises the profile and background of the company.

Profile and Background - *Consultancy Services*	
Brief overview of the firm's activities, its mission and focus	
Industry	European Project Management
Technology	Project Management software
Product/service	Training and consultancy
Market and targeted customers	Wales, Romania, Poland, Hungary, Lithuania, Bulgaria and other European countries
Company's current mission and focus	To develop the company at a European level over the next three years.

Table 7.1: Consultancy Services

The company has grown on an incremental basis and this followed a long period of time to receive approval with the University. The construction of the Web site, which was essential to the operation of the company, took six months and this was achieved on 1st March 2005. The company has won a number of contracts and this has therefore not been an issue. It has also been important to have clients returning and to draw on their expertise. There are six current clients including public sector and voluntary organisations.

Energy Management Systems

Energy Management Systems (EMS) was launched in January 2005 as a spinout company. The focus of the company is to reduce utility costs and to provide customised online utility information regarding these costs and to ensure that they remain low. The company works with customers to provide a full energy/utility service ranging from fuel purchasing, meter installation, advanced monitoring and targeting to project engineering and information technology (IT) solutions. In its early stages the company received public support through the Spinout programme and more recent developments have been resourced by the founders. In addition to IT and software developments, EMS undertakes remote analysis of customers' consumption patterns and works closely with clients to achieve reduced costs. The company aims to be a professional service provider by establishing trust through building personal relationships with customers over the Internet. This has been included in the firm's overall marketing and e-business strategy. Through this trust it enables EMS to work with customers, employing the most appropriate technology to gain outstanding results. The products and services provided include metering hardware and connectivity; IT support, hosting, VDN and networking; installation of metering hardware and network cabling; installation of gas, water and steam meters; Web design, Web development and consultancy. Table 7.2 summarises the profile and background of the company.

Profile and Background - *Energy Management Systems*	
Brief overview of the firm's activities, its mission and focus	
Industry	Energy
Technology	Energy management technology
Product/service	.Net Web management system
Market and targeted customers	Public, private and leisure organisations
Company's current mission and focus	To maintain and consolidate company activities over the next five years.

Table 7.2: Energy Management Systems

Literary Book Publishing

Literary Book Publishing (LBP) was launched, and registered, as a limited company in May 2001 as a spinout company from the University with public support through the Spinout programme. The company publishes short stories by authors in a small book format and provides retailing through coffee shops, tearooms, restaurants and hotels. The books are being marketed, over the Internet, to customers in the United Kingdom (UK), United States (US) initially and the English speaking world due to the co-founders' business partner being American. This role of the Internet has been included in the company's overall marketing and e-business strategy. Other markets and languages will be considered later. There is a three-year business plan targeting sales in the UK and USA for the first three years. The spin off is linked to the University since both of the co-founders are graduates of the English Department Centre for Creative Writing. This provides a link with academics and a network of authors. The co-founders are MPhil students from the University. Table 7.3 summarises the profile and background of the company.

Profile and Background - *Literary Book Publishing*	
Brief overview of the firm's activities, its mission and focus	
Industry	Book Publishing
Technology	Book publishing graphic design technology
Product/service	A6 pocket sized books
Market and targeted customers	UK, USA and the English speaking world
Company's current mission and focus	To develop the company in the book publishing trade over the next three years.

Table 7.3: Literary Book Publishing

The initial markets are in the UK and America to be followed internationally. Work with partners is finite for international distribution. Once the product is proved LBP will approach international chains such as Marks and Spencer. As a small start-up company they are not ready to sell to Marks and Spencer who have 6 warehouses and 140 coffee shops in the UK. The large international chain stores will consider the product once it is proven. A contact for London and Cambridge has taken the books to shops that are willing to pay a higher price. The product will sell better in the South East of England and it is hoped that this will be the case with international markets. The company organised a short story competition for authors on its Web site for the winners and runners-up to have their first books published. There are also competitions for poetry and writing for children.

Mobile Phone Security

The Mobile Phone Security (MPS) company is a spinout of the University with limited public support through the Spinout programme. It was formed in 2004 by the Founder who as an undergraduate developed a unique patent pending software application which overcomes password protection technology limitations. The application is different to existing mobile security software since it is undetectable. This provides high levels of data security since there is no evidence that data is hidden. Once the application is installed in a mobile phone it creates a second menu for users to store confidential contact information, office documents, pictures or video files. These are safe since there is no trace of the second menu which is not visible in the event of unauthorised use, theft or loss. Since the menu mirrors standard phone functionality it is easy for the user to navigate requiring little effort to learn.

Since the take up of 3G services has not been as strong as the industry forecast companies are looking for third party content to differentiate between their own and competitors' service and product offerings. This will result in third party software developers such as MPS to be in a strong position. It is envisaged that the primary route to the OEM market will be through regional licensing agreements with major network operators. Through the pre-installation of the software in phones this will enable users to experience the software application and will allow the encouragement of new potential users through direct marketing by the network operators. In order to encourage new users to adopt the service the try before you buy approach is a powerful tactic.

The ability to differentiate the network operators' product offering, for example the incorporation of e-mail facilities and second secure message facilities for secure contacts, will relative to the downloadable version also allow a premium price. End user pricing of the network provider is expected to be in the range of £9 to £12 a year. As well as repeat business for the network operators each time a user upgrades a phone the software application will generate considerable new revenue streams. It is also anticipated that the software, with time phased licence agreements and enhanced product differentiation, will enable network operators to increase their market share through regional exclusivity rights and to further increase revenue. Table 7.4 summarises the profile and background of the company.

Profile and Background - *Mobile Phone Security*	
Brief overview of the firm's activities, its mission and focus	
Industry	Data security industry
Technology	Mobile phone technology
Product/service	Application software
Market and targeted customers	Global
Company's current mission and focus	To develop the company in the data security industry over the next three years.

Table 7.4: Mobile Phone Security

Pet Care

The founder started-up as an incorporated company in May 2004, using Spinout programme public support, with a new product that needed development following considerable research into the market. When the company was at the early development stage there was a need for a manufacturer. It was difficult to find early stage support since contacts were reluctant to provide backing and were cautious. The original idea arose from outside the University from a company formed by the founder in 1986. This produced water beds for pets and a cage system as a holding bay for animals before and after hospital. Collaborative work originally took place with another University. The bed, for use in animal hospitals, was new on the market and with this product it was the first time the founder had started a company. From the experience of doing this the founder decided to start a company again.

With the present company the first product is an outside cat cabin, which is being marketed on the company Web site. This has been developed following the founder's experience of housing cats while at work. There is a clear demand arising from owners not being able to have a cat flap in a wall, or where the cost to replace a door is prohibitive (@ £800 in some cases). From this the idea for a cat cabin arose. Table 7.5 summarises the profile and background of the company.

Profile and Background - *Pet Care*	
Brief overview of the firm's activities, its mission and focus	
Industry	Pet products
Technology	Pet care technologies
Product/service	Specialised pet care products – cat house, pet bed and animal warm mattress.
Market and targeted customers	UK (in the first year) – pet super stores, multiple retailers, pet shops, privately owned high street outlets, veterinary surgeries. Europe (second year). North American market (third year).
Company's current mission and focus	Through the development and sale of pet products the company will establish itself in the UK market and progress to the European and United States markets.

Table 7.5: Pet Care

In the first year the company concentrated on the UK and Irish markets. Since this was a challenge it was decided to concentrate on one product. In the second year the company sold into the European, United States and Chinese markets. The Chinese market is a large window of opportunity since the majority of homes have a cat and therefore there is an immense market. Since the cat house is a unique shape representing the head of cat at the entrance it looks good. It is therefore functional since the cat head fits into the garden as a piece of furniture and appears as an attractive product to customers on the company Web site. This was taken into account in the overall marketing and e-business strategy.

Under Grad

Under Grad is a company, which provides a scheme that encourages companies to employ the best engineering and technology students through the company's Web site. The co-founders started the company about seven years ago in January 2003 with public support through the Spinout programme. The idea for the company arose due to the national decline in the number of students gaining employment in the areas of engineering and technology. Following this being recognised as an opportunity in 2002, a limited company was formed in January 2003. Office space was provided at the University spin-off premises with the help of the Head of the University Commercial Services. The ambition of the founders is to help the University and other universities (like minded organisations and departments) to find industrial employment for their engineering and technology students. The two founders are both employed by the University in the School of Technology and when they formed the company they were the two directors. Office space, support staff and facilities are provided in the School, as well as the office space at the University spin-off premises. Table 7.6 summarises the profile and background of the company.

Profile and Background - *Under Grad*	
Brief overview of the firm's activities, its mission and focus	
Industry	Employment
Technology	Student employment systems
Product/service	Employment service for companies to employ engineering and technology students.
Market and targeted customers	• Engineering and technology students • Companies • Universities
Company's current mission and focus	To maintain and consolidate company activities in the employment of engineering and technology students over the next five years.

Table 7.6: Under Grad

The company was developed within the University's School of Technology. The firm places undergraduate students at a host company while studying part-time for a degree using the Web site. Two days are spent by trainees at the University and the rest of the week at work. Complex systems have been developed to support the scheme, by a franchise centre, through innovative support systems with the award of the ISO 9000:2000 accreditation of the work. Originally work was aimed at higher education institutions in Britain, but following modification overseas colleges and a private European training organisation have become involved. Franchise centres deliver key skills modules at level 1 through to five-year supported programmes. The company provides valuable work experience to students during their university course, with no fees and a bursary up to £9,000. Businesses benefit from motivated undergraduates studying at university, working with the businesses, and they become competent and experienced company members. Franchise centres are cost effective. These have been very successful and have helped to reverse trends in declining numbers and entry qualifications for engineering and technology students. There have also been follow-on efforts such as the retention of students. Through students being more aware of potential debt, and the incentive of a bursary and work experience they are attracted to the scheme.

Conclusions

Since most of the global start-up companies are fairly young they have tended to report early stage development in terms of business growth. It is, therefore, planned to undertake follow-up interviews in future years to develop a longitudinal study to reveal business developments. In order to do this a coherent structure for both the data and the analysis will be essential.

Recommended Reading

Thomas, B., Brooksbank, D. and Thompson, R. (2009) Optimising the regional infrastructure for higher education global start-ups in Wales, *International Journal of Globalisation and Small Business*, 3(2), pp. 220-237.

References

Amin, A. (2000) Organisational learning through communities of practice, paper presented at the *Millennium Schumpeter Conference*, University of Manchester, Manchester, June/July.

Asheim, B.T., Isaksen, A. (2002) Regional Innovation Systems: The Integration Of Local 'Sticky' And Global 'Ubiquitous' Knowledge, *Journal of Technology Transfer*, 27, pp. 77-86.

Autio, E. and Sapienza, H.J. (2000) Comparing process and born global perspectives in the international growth of technology-based new firms, *Frontiers of Entrepreneurship Research*, Centre for Entrepreneurial Studies, Babson College, pp. 413-424.

Autio, E., Sapienza, H.J. and Almeida, J.G. (2000) Effects of age at entry, knowledge intensity and imitability on international growth, *Academy of Management Journal*, 43(5), pp. 090-924.

Bell, J. (1995) The internationalisation of small computer software firms: a further challenge to "stage" theories, *European Journal of Marketing*, 29(8), pp. 60-75.

Bristow, G. (2005) Everyone's a 'winner': problematising the discourse of regional competitiveness, *Journal of Economic Geography*, 5, pp. 285-304.

Brooksbank, D. and Thomas, B. (2000) *Assessing the Challenges and Requirements of Higher Education Spinout Enterprises*, Detailed interviews with spinout companies, Section 2 WDA Report, 68 pages, August.

Brooksbank, D., Thomas, B., Miller, C. and Thompson, R. (2006) *Generic regional support infrastructure schema for global higher education spinout start-ups*, GlobalStart project report, IPS2001-41038, June.

Bunnell, T.G. and Coe, N.M. (2001) Spaces and scales of innovation, *Progress in Human Geography*, 25, pp. 569–589.

Burgel, O. and Murray, G.C. (2000) The international market entry choices of start-yup companies in high-technology industries, *Journal of International Marketing*, 8(2), pp. 33-62.

Cooke, P. (2001) *Strategies for Regional Innovation Systems: Learning Transfer and Applications*, UNIDO World Industrial Development Report (WIDR).

Coviello, N.E. and Munro, H.J. (1995) Growing the entrepreneurial firm: networking for international market development, *European Journal of Marketing*, 297, pp. 49-61.

Doloreux, D. (2002) What we should know about regional systems of innovation, *Technology and Society*, 24, pp. 243-263.

Finance Wales (2001) *Investing in the future of Wales: Funding and Management Support*, Cardiff, financewales.

Freel, M. (2003) Sectoral patterns of small firm innovation, networking and proximity, *Research Policy*, 32(5), pp. 751-770.

Gertler, M. (2001) Tacit Knowledge and the Economic Geography of Context or the Undefinable Tacitness of Being (There), paper presented at the *Nelson and Winter DRUID Summer Conference*, Aalborg, Denmark, June.

Gibbs, D., Jonas, A., Reiner, S. and Spooner, D. (2001) Governance, institutional capacity and partnerships in local economic development: theoretical issues and empirical evidence from the Humber Sub-region, *Transactions of the Institute of British Geography*, 26, pp. 103-119.

Harveston, P.D. (2000) *Synoptic versus incremental internationalisation: An examination of born global and gradual globalising firms*, Unpublished Doctoral Dissertation, The University of Memphis.

Howells, J. (1999) Regional systems of innovation. In D. Archibugi, J.Howells and J.Michie (eds.) *Innovation policy in a global economy*, pp. 67-93, Cambridge University Press, Cambridge.

Hospers, G.J. and Beugelsdijk, S. (2002), Regional cluster policies: learning by comparing?, *KYKLOS: International Review for Social Sciences*, 55(3), pp. 381-402

Knight, G.A. and Cavusgil (1996) The born global firm: a challenge to traditional internationalisation theory. In S.T.Cavusgil and T.K.Madsen (eds.) *Export internationalising research – enrichment and challenges*, Advances in International Marketing, 8, 11-26, NY: JAI Press Inc.

Lagendijk, A. (2003) Scaling knowledge production: how significant is the region? In M.M.Fischer and J.Frohling, *Knowledge, Complexity and Innvoation Systems, Advances in spatial science*, Spinger-Verlag, Berlin, pp. 79-100.

Lagendijk, A. and Cornford, J. (2000) Regional institutions and knowledge – tracking new forms of regional policy, *Geoforum*, 31, pp. 209-218.

Lawton-Smith, H. Tracey, P. and Clark, G. (2003) European Policy and the Regions: A Review and Analysis of Tensions, *European Planning Studies*, 11(7), October.

Lift (1998) *Financing Innovation: A Guide, Linking Innovation, Finance and Technology*, Luxembourg, European Commission.

Lovering, J. (1999) Theory led by Policy: The Inadequacies of the "New Regionalism" (Illustrated from the Case of Wales), *International Journal for Urban and Regional Research*, 23(2), pp. 379-395.

Lovering, J. (2001) The Coming Regional Crisis (and how to avoid it), *Regional Studies*, 35, pp. 349-354.
Lumpkin, G.T. and Dess, G.G. (1996) Clarifying the entrepreneurial orientation construct and linking it to performance, *Academy of Management Review*, 21(1), pp. 135-172.

Lumpkin, G.T. (1998) Do new entrant firms have an entrepreneurial orientation? Paper presented at the *annual meeting of the Academy of Management*, San Diego, CA.

Mackinnon, D., Cumbers, A. and Chapman, K. (2002) Learning, innovation and regional development: a critical appraisal of recent debates, *Progress in Human Geography*, 26(3), pp. 293-311.

MacLeod, G. (2001) New Regionalism Reconsidered: Globalisation and the Remaking of Political nomic Space, *International Journal of Urban and Regional Research*, 25(4).

Madsen, T.K. and Servais, P. (1997) The Internationalisation of Born Globals: an Evolutionary Process? *International Business Review*, 6(6), pp. 561-583.

Madsen, T.K., Rasmussen, E.S. and Servais, P. (2000) Differences and similarities between born globals and other types of exporters. In A. Yaprak and J. Tutek (eds.) *Globalisation, the multinational form and emerging economies, Advances in International Marketing*, 10, pp. 247-265, Amsterdam: JAI/Elsevier Inc.

Mamis, R.A. (1989) *Global start-up*, Inc., Aug.: 38-47.

Martin, R. and Sunley, P. (2003) Deconstructing clusters: chaotic concept or policy panacea? *Journal of Economic Geography*, 3, pp. 5-35

McDougall, P.P. and Oviatt, B.M. (1996) New venture internationalisation, strategic change and performance: a follow-up study, *Journal of Business Venturing*, 11(1), pp. 23-40.

Metcalfe, S. Ramlogan, R. and Uyarra, E. (2003) Competition, Innovation and Development: the Instituted Connection, *Institutions and Economic Development*, 1(1).

Moulaert, F. and Sekia, F. (2003) Territorial innovation models: a critical survey, *Regional Studies*, 37, pp. 289-302.

Oviatt, B.M. and McDougall, P. (1994) Toward a theory of international new ventures, *Journal of International Business Studies*, 25(1), pp. 45-64.

Oviatt, B.M. and McDougall, P. (1995) Global start-ups: entrepreneurs on a worldwide stage, *Academy of Management Executive*, 9(2), pp. 30-43.

Oviatt, B.M. and McDougall, P.P. (1997) Challenges for internationalisation process theory: the case of international new ventures, *Management International Review*, 37(2) (Special Issue), pp. 85-99.

Oxford Innovation (1998) *Technology Exploitation Guide: for Universities and Research Institutes*, Oxford: OI Ltd.

Radosevic, S. (2002) Regional Innovation Systems in Central and Eastern Europe: Determinants, Organisers and Alignments, *Journal of Technology Transfer*, 27, pp. 87-96.

Randles, S. and Dicken, P. (2004) 'Scale' and the instituted construction of the urban: contrasting the cases of Manchester and Lyon, *Environment and Planning A*, 36(11), pp. 2011-2032.

Rasmussen, E.S. and Madsen, T.K. (2002) The born global concept, Paper presented in the *28th EIBA Conference 2002* (Athens, Greece).

Ray, D.M. (1989) Strategic Implications of Entrepreneurial Ventures "Born International": Four Case Studies, Paper Frontiers in Entrepreneurship Research, *Babson-Kauffman Entrepreneurial Research Conference* (BKERC).

Rennie, M. (1993) *Global competitiveness: born global*, McKinsey Quarterly, 4, pp. 45-52.

Rialp-Criado, A., Rialp-Criado, J. and Knight, G.A. (2002) *The Phenomenon of International New Ventures, Global Start-ups, and Born-Globals: What do we know after a Decade (1993-2002) of exhaustive Scientific Inquiry?* Working Paper, Department d'Economia de l'Empresa, Universitat Autònoma de Barcelon, Barcelona.

Roberts, E.B. and Senturia, T.A. (1996) Globalising the emerging high-technology company, *Industrial Marketing Management*, 25, pp. 491-506.

Saarenketo, S. (2002) *Born Globals – Internationalisation of Small and Medium-Sized Knowledge-Intensive Firms*, Doctoral Dissertation Lappeenranta University of Technology, Finland.

Servais, P. and Rasmussen, E.S. (2000) Different types of international new ventures. Paper presented at the *Academy of International Business (AIB) Annual Meeting*, November, Phoenix, AZ, USA, pp. 1-27.

Thomas, B., Packham, G. and Miller, C.J. (2006) Technological innovation, entrepreneurship, higher education and economic regeneration in Wales: a policy study, *Industry and Higher Education*, 20(6), pp. 433-440.

Thomas, B., Miller, C., Simmons, G. and Packham, G. (2008) The Role of Web sites and E-commerce in the development of Global Start-ups. In F.Zhao (ed.), *Handbook of Research on Information Technology Entrepreneurship and Innovation*, Idea Group, Hershey, In Press.

Uyarra, E. (2005) Knowledge, *Diversity and Regional Innovation Policies: Theoretical Issues and Empirical Evidence of Regional Innovation Strategies*, PREST Discussion Paper Series, Institute of Innovation Research, University of Manchester, Manchester, 1-18.

Wakkee, I, van der Sijde, P. and Kirwan, P. (2003) *An Empirical Exploration of the Global Startup Concept in an Entrepreneurship Context*, GS Leuven, Working Paper.

Zahira, S.A., Ireland, R.D. and Hitt, M.A. (2000) International expansion by new firms: international diversity, mode of entry, technological learning and performance, *Academy of Management Journal*, 43(5), pp. 925-950.

8. Innovation Performance Indicators

"A manager is responsible for the application and performance of knowledge."
PETER DRUCKER (1909-2005)

This chapter at a glance:

- Introduction: innovation performance indicators and small firms
- Innovation performance
- Framework for measuring innovation performance
- Regional Innovation Performance
- Conclusions

Introduction: innovation performance indicators and small firms

In the 1990s small firms were seen as a driving force for job creation, growth and global competitiveness through innovation (Feldman et al, 2002). According to Freudenberg (2003, p. 14) "innovation can be defined as the development, deployment and economic utilisation of new products, processes and services, and is an increasingly important contributor to sustained and sustainable economic growth, both at micro-economic and macro-economic levels". One of the main indicators cited in the literature used to measure innovation in small firms is research and development (R&D) (Mueller, 1967; Grabowski, 1968; Mansfield, 1968). Other measures include patents (Hall, Griliches and Hausman, 1986; Pakes and Griliches, 1980; Scherer, 1965; 1983; Schwalbach and Zimmermann, 1991), new product innovations (Acs and Audretsch, 1990; 1993; Audretsch, 1995) and the adoption of advanced manufacturing technologies (Dunne, 1994; Romeo, 1975; Siegel, 1999). With regard to these it has been found that large firms have a greater propensity to patent than small firms, small firms appear to be as innovative as large firms and large and small firm innovative activities appear to be complementary (Feldman et al, 2002). A summary of the findings from selected literature on firm size and innovation performance indicators is shown in Table 8.1.

The differences between large and small firms with regard to innovation can be explained through the model of the knowledge production function (Griliches, 1979). A simplified production function can be expanded to include the stock of knowledge as an input and an investment in knowledge that many firms will make will be R&D (Feldman et al, 2002). The OECD Frascati Manual (OECD, 1997) defines R&D as "creative work undertaken on a systematic basis in order to increase the stock of knowledge, including knowledge of man, culture and society, and the use of this stock of knowledge to devise new applications". There will be other activities that generate knowledge and although many small firms will not undertake R&D they will still be innovative and these firms will depend on knowledge spillovers from external sources including universities (Audretsch and Feldman, 1996a&b; Link and Rees, 1990). In fact, small firms when compared with large firms will be better at absorbing knowledge from external sources (Feldman et al, 2002). Here new employees will be important and small firms will be able to exploit knowledge embodied in employees to a greater degree than large firms (Audretsch and Stephan, 1996). The reason for this is that small firms will provide an environment for their workers to develop ideas not apparent in large firms (Prevezer, 1997).

this is well established. A more complete compilation of such simple indicators has been undertaken by Freudenberg (2003). This chapter identifies those indicators of innovation performance that are relevant to small firm policy which enables comparison of innovation activity between regions/countries.

Comparison of innovation performance with a set of countries and regions enables greater in-depth study with regard to small firm innovation policy. The identification of innovation and technology diffusion as a long term micro-driver of productivity and growth has been identified by the OECD (2001). The aim of the chapter is to seek to answer the question "what are the most appropriate innovation performance indicators for small firms to enable accurate comparison of innovation activity between countries and regions".

Innovation performance

The literature on innovation performance indicators considers the development of measures used to assess trends over time in order to compare the performance of countries at national, regional and industry levels. Grupp (2006) has described innovation indicators as "statistics that describe various aspects of innovation. Individual indicators are generally partial, that is, they do not measure innovation as a whole. Collections of selected indicators are used to measure innovation more broadly. Innovation indicators are often indirect because the underlying phenomenon of interest, innovation, is intangible or not directly observable." This chapter therefore provides a selective overview of the literature with regard to the different approaches adopted including the use of composite indicators with special reference to small firms. Veugelers (2005) has provided an analysis of appropriate indicators for the European Commission (EC) using the concept of national innovative capacity (NIC) (Table 8.2) which is defined as the "ability of a nation to not only produce ideas, but also to commercialise a flow of innovative technologies over the longer term" (Sharpe and Guilbaud, 2005). This approach cautions the use of individual statistical indicators to assess national innovation performance and suggests a systemic approach between indicators and socio economic development (Sharpe and Guilbaud, 2005).

Characteristic	Measure
Common innovation infrastructure – cross cutting institutions, resources and policies	Existing stock of technological know how
	Supporting basic research and higher education
	Overall science and technology policy
Technology Cluster Specific Conditions	Technology specific know how – specialised R&D personnel
	Incentives for innovation – lead users, intellectual property rights (IPR) and market competition
	Related supporting industries (clusters)
Quality of links between clusters and common factors	Industry-science relationships
	Efficient labour and capital markets

Table 8.2: National Innovation Capacity Source: Veugelers (2005, pp 8-9)

A European Innovation Scoreboard (EIS) (Table 8.3) has been developed with regard to the drivers and output of innovation and from this an industry dimension for many indicators can be developed (Sharpe and Guilbaud, 2005). The robustness of innovation scoreboards has been criticised empirically by heuristic type analysis (Grupp and Mogee, 2004). Further to this Veugelers notes that there needs to be care taken with inter industry comparisons of innovation indicators and since the systemic approach to innovation is at the technology sectoral level innovation performance should be analysed across sectors (the lack of data at the sectoral level is the challenge) (Veugelers, 2005).

Public R&D expenditures (GERD-BERD)	% of GDP	OECD
Business expenditures on R&D (BERD)	% of GDP	OECD
High-tech patent applications	Per million population	EUROSTAT
High-tech patents granted	Per million population	EUROSTAT
Patent applications	Per million population	EUROSTAT
Patents granted	Per million population	EUROSTAT
Transmission and application of knowledge		
SMEs innovating in-house	% of all SMEs	EUROSTAT
SMEs involved in innovation cooperation	% of all SMEs	EUROSTAT
Innovation expenditures	% of total turnover	EUROSTAT
SMEs using non technological change	% of all SMEs	EUROSTAT
Innovation finance, output and markets		
Share of high-tech venture capital investment		EVCA
Share of early stage venture capital in GDP		EUROSTAT
Sales of 'new to market' products	% of total turnover	EUROSTAT
Sales of 'new to the firm but not new to the market' products	% of total turnover	EUROSTAT
Internet access		EUROSTAT
ICT expenditures	% of GDP	EUROSTAT
Share of manufacturing value-added in high-tech sectors		EUROSTAT

Table 8.3: European Innovation Scoreboard
Sources: EU Trend Chart (2004), Veugelers (2005, pp 15-16)

In a study for Industry Canada the Conference Board of Canada (CBC, 2004) published "Exploring Canada's Innovation Character: Benchmarking Against Global Best" as part of the innovation strategy for the federal government. The framework provided by the Conference Board for innovation benchmarking divides innovation into the four aspects of knowledge performance, skills performance, innovation environment and community based innovation (Sharpe and Guilbaud, 2005). The framework is composed of seventeen indicators including the indicator of business expenditure on R&D (BERD) as a % of GDP which allows a comparison of R&D activity for industries and countries and the R&D statistics follow definitions provided by the Frascati model (OECD, 1997). The measurement of patents also enables an understanding of innovation performance since they indicate the creation and transfer of knowledge (Sharpe and Guilbaud, 2005). If a patent is filed at the European Patent Office, Japanese Patent Office and the United States Patent Office at the same time it is considered to be a member of a triadic patent family (Stead, 2001). More generally the most common indicator of innovation is gross expenditure on R&D (GERD) as a % of GDP (Sharpe and Guilbaud, 2005).

At the level of the small and medium-sized enterprise (SME), or the individual project, management practices such as scoreboarding or benchmarking have been established (for industrial innovation patent scoreboards and R&D scoreboards are published) (Grupp, 2006). Furthermore, at national levels, approaches include common procedures to calculate composite indicators. According to Freudenberg (2003, p. 3) "composite indicators are synthetic indices of individual indicators and are increasingly being used to rank countries in various performance and policy areas". Moreover, Freudenberg (2003, p. 7), in developing a theoretical framework, notes that "composite indicators are generally used to summarise a number of underlying individual indicators or variables. An indicator is a quantitative or qualitative measure derived from a series of observed facts that can reveal relative position in a given area and, when measured over time, can point out the direction of change. ... There are basically three levels of groupings: 1) Individual indicator sets represents a menu of separate indicators or statistics. ... 2) Thematic indicators are individual indicators which are grouped together around a specific area or theme. ... 3) Composite indicators are formed when thematic indicators are compiled into a synthetic index and presented as a single composite measure." This work is being led by the European Commission (EC, 2003) who are using composite indicators to aggregate the different indicators into "simpler constructs for the purpose of summarising multi-dimensional phenomena" (Grupp, 2006). Through aggregating different variables the "big picture" is summarised with regard to a many dimensional issue (EC, 2003). The European Innovation Scoreboard (EIS, 2009) has been published on a regular basis since 2000 using composite indicators (Grupp, 2006). In 2002 the EC Joint Research Centre published a report on composite indicator development (Saisana and Tarantola, 2002). This was followed by publication of the manual "Tools for Composite Indicators Building" (guidelines for the construction of composite indicators have been published by the European Commission and OECD) (Nardo et al., 2005a&b).

In 2001 the European Innovation Scoreboard (EC, 2001) presented eighteen indicators including R&D intensity, business expenditures on R&D, European and US patents, SMEs' innovation and co-operation and innovation intensity. A tentative Summary Innovation Index (SII) was constructed for the indicators within the UK (score 4.4) ranked fourth (Grupp, 2006). There have been further releases of the EIS (EC, 2003, 2005) with the methodology altered for the composite number. In relation to methodology Freudenberg (2003, pp. 9-10) notes the problem of data deletion, missing values and other indicator development problems (metric scales include "distance from the best and worst performers", "minimum-maximum approach", "leader and laggard", unreliability due to outliers and "re-scaling") (Grupp, 2006). More sophisticated procedures of weighting are randomly assigned weights although these do not solve the problem of arbitrariness (Freudenberg, 2003, p. 25). Problems when calculating composite indicators require a thorough investigation of robustness (Freudenberg, 2003, p. 13) and examples include heuristic approaches (Grupp and Mogee, 2004), linear and non-linear programming methods (Schubert, 2006) and Monte Carlo simulation methods (Freudenberg, 2003, p. 25). Grupp and Mogee (2004) have also noted "country tuning" with composition procedures intentionally placing certain countries in a better position than others. The problems of missing values also affect composite indicators (the range of composite indices for indicators of innovation performance can show considerable variation between countries) (Freudenberg, 2003, p. 9). It is anticipated that accuracy and quality of composite indicators will improve with advances in the collection of data and the development of indicators although it is suggested that there should be pragmatism with regard to the implementation of composites (Freudenberg, 2003).

From the literature a framework can be identified (Table 8.4) that develops a composite of innovation performance for selecting and placing indicators which combine three to five underlying variables predominantly derived from OECD databases (OECD, 2001).

Performance area	Generation of new knowledge	Industry-science linkages	Industrial innovation
Indicators	Basic research	Government or higher education R&D financed by business	Business enterprise R&D (BERD)
	R&D performance by non-business sector	Scientific papers cited in patents	Business researchers
	Non-business researchers	Publications in most industry-relevant scientific disciplines	Number of patents in "triadic" patent families
	PhD graduation rates in science, engineering and health		Firms with new or improved products or processes
	Scientific and technical articles		

Table 8.4: Framework for identifying indicators to measure innovation performance
Sources: OECD (2001); Freudenberg (2003)

The first performance area (generation of new knowledge) includes basic research as a % of GDP, R&D performance by non-business sector, non-business researchers, PhD graduation rates, scientific and technical articles; the second (industry-science linkages) involves data concerning R&D, patents and publications; and the third (industrial innovation) concerns data regarding business research, patents, new products and processes (OECD, 2001; Freudenberg, 2003).

Framework for measuring innovation performance

In order to develop innovation performance indicators of relevance to small firms there are two principal stages. The first stage is developing a framework for selecting and placing indicators in three performance areas according to i) basic research and the production of new knowledge, ii) links between public and private research and iii) levels of industrial innovation (OECD, 2001). The second stage concerning the selection of variables and indicators involves investigation of the three performance areas outlined in stage 1. Variables are derived from databases including those of the EC and OECD. The core components include the generation of new knowledge (involving variables such as basic research as a percentage of GDP and non-business researchers in the labour force), industry-science linkages (business financed R&D performed by government and higher education as a percentage of GDP, patents and publications), and industrial innovation (business enterprise R&D (BERD) as a percentage of GDP, business researchers in the labour force, patents and new products and processes) (Freudenberg, 2003). Through categorisation and weighting, indicators can be determined to measure innovation performance.

By reviewing the current innovation performance indicators identified in the literature those that are relevant to small firms are illustrated. For this initial work the underlying variables for the three core components (Table 8.4) have been simplified according to the data available in order to undertake the initial analysis. Therefore, for the performance areas of 1) the generation of new knowledge, 2) industry-science linkages and 3) industrial innovation underlying variables include 1.1) basic research, 1.2) public R&D, 2.1) med/high tech employment in manufacturing, 2.2) high-tech patent applications, 3.1) business R&D and 3.2) patent applications (Table 8.5).

Performance area	Generation of new knowledge	Industry-science linkages	Industrial innovation
Indicators	Basic research	Med/High tech employment in manufacturing	Business R&D
	Public R&D	High-tech patent applications	Patent applications

Table 8.5: An initial framework for identifying indicators relevant to small firms

The approach used in this chapter to provide an analysis of innovation activity for comparison with other countries and regions, uses the initial framework (Table 8.5) and considers performance area and underlying variables (indicators) for a national/regional profile according to high, moderate and low levels of activity.

UK regional innovation indicator data has been considered in relation to the EU Regional Innovation Scoreboard (RIS) (EC, 2003). From this it has been possible to formulate regional innovation performance and to determine those indicators relevant to small firms.

Regional Innovation Performance

The development of innovation performance indicators to compare countries and regions involves standardising and weighting variables. The variables selected will have to be normalised to enable comparison. Although the influences of the standardisation method on the results of performance indicators are limited the weighting of variables strongly influence indicators. The results show how the three components described in stage 2 contribute to aggregated measures. This gives an idea to the overall innovation performance of small firms and shows the national strengths and weaknesses at the indicator level.

The results are based on the two Regional Innovation Scoreboards published in 2002 and 2003 under the European Commission's European Trend Chart on Innovation (EU Trend Chart, 2002; 2003). This is supplemented with findings from the 2006 European Regional Innovation Scoreboard (EU Trend Chart, 2006). In comparison with the European Innovation Scoreboard for the twenty five European Union states in 2006 the reports in 2002 and 2003 focused on regional innovation performance of the fifteen European Union states using a more limited number of indicators (EU Trend Chart, 2006). Whereas the number of regions increased from 173 in 2003 to 208 in 2006 there was a decrease from 13 to 7 in the number of indicators (EU Trend Chart, 2003; 2006). In order to determine the level of regional analysis the Nomenclature of Territorial Units for Statistics (NUTS) classification is used (OECD, 2007).

For the 2006 European Regional Innovation Scoreboard (EU Trend Chart, 2006) regional data are determined using two indexes one of which is the Regional National Summary Innovation Index (RNSII) which can be expressed:

$$RNSII = \sum_{j=1}^{m} x_{ijkt}^{n}$$

where x_{ijkt} is the value of indicator i for region j in country k and time t and m is the number of indicators for which regional data are available.

The Regional European Summary Innovation Index (REUSII) can be expressed:

$$REUSII = \sum_{j=1}^{m} x_{ijkt}^{eu}$$

The Revealed Regional Summary Innovation Index (RRSII) is calculated as the weighted average of the re-scaled values for RNSII and REUSII as follows:

$$RRSII = ¾ * REUSII + ¼ * RNSII$$

Using the measure of RRSII UK regional innovation performance is shown in Table 8.6.

Rank	UK Region	Average
12	South East	0.72
17	Eastern	0.69
35	London	0.59
37	South West	0.58
42	West Midlands	0.57
47	East Midlands	0.57
56	North West	0.54
72	Yorkshire and The Humber	0.49
78	North East	0.48
80	Wales	0.48
89	Scotland	0.45
113	Northern Ireland	0.41

Table 8.6: UK Regional Innovation Performance 2006 Source: EU Trend Chart (2006)

This shows the ranking for UK regions with the South East of England highest for the UK and Scotland and Northern Ireland below Wales. Table 8.7 shows the impact on UK regions' EU ranks from changes in methodology for calculating the composite innovation index between 2002 and 2006 (EU Trend Chart, 2006).

	RIS 2002		RIS 2003		RIS 2006			
Transformation	NO		NO		YES		YES	
Re-scaling	NO		YES		YES		YES	
National weight	1/2		1/2		1/2		1/4	
Region	RRSII	Rank	RRSII	Rank	RRSII	Rank	RRSII	Rank
East Midlands	107	52	0.36	55	0.53	50	0.57	47
Eastern	147	18	0.5	18	0.66	18	0.69	17
London	112	42	0.41	38	0.56	40	0.59	35
North East	86	94	0.29	85	0.44	89	0.48	78
North West	102	65	0.34	68	0.5	61	0.54	56
Northern Ireland	72	134	0.23	131	0.37	129	0.41	113
Scotland	92	85	0.33	73	0.4	107	0.45	89
South East	150	14	0.54	15	0.69	12	0.72	12
South West	109	46	0.38	48	0.54	42	0.58	37
Wales	86	96	0.3	82	0.43	91	0.48	80
West Midlands	108	48	0.38	47	0.54	47	0.57	42
Yorkshire and The Humber	90	87	0.3	83	0.45	83	0.49	72

Table 8.7: Impact on UK regions' EU ranks from changes in methodology
Source: EU Trend Chart (2006)

In 2002 a simple methodology was used with data not transformed or re-scaled and national and European components receiving equal weighting (EU Trend Chart, 2002). For 2003 re-scaling of indicators was introduced and five indicators from the 2nd Community Innovation Survey (CIS) were included (EU Trend Chart, 2003). 2006 introduced the transformation of data with square root transformation for five indicators and double square root transformation for two indicators (a smaller weight for the national component of ¼ instead of ½ is used in 2006) (EU Trend Chart, 2006). The EU Regional Innovation Scoreboard 2006 UK data are shown in Table 8.8 for T-2, T-1 and T.

Relative to EU	HRSTC			LIFE-LONG			MED/HI-TEC			HI-TECH			PUB R&D			BUS R&D			PATENTS		
	T-2	T-1	T	T-2	T-1	T	T-2	T-1	T	T-2	T-1	T	T-2	T-1	T	T-2	T-1	T	T-2	T-1	T
United Kingdom	121	119	119	281	277	266	98	103	105	138	145	142	89	89	93	98	103	103	95	97	94
East Midlands	101	99	99	266	254	257	116	124	117	122	123	112	61	61	58	127	121	122	73	87	90
Eastern	114	109	109	286	281	269	111	110	109	165	179	174	91	91	99	274	272	276	178	189	174
London	161	155	155	325	327	308	36	39	40	192	215	188	89	89	90	35	35	34	122	120	117
North East	88	96	96	254	248	230	129	131	135	97	143	108	56	56	55	42	45	52	48	49	65
North West	105	114	114	267	276	259	105	118	117	111	105	130	52	52	51	124	133	121	71	73	74
Northern Ireland	119	101	101	187	182	162	84	78	79	80	82	86	56	56	54	53	40	36	26	26	19
Scotland	132	126	126	270	255	240	84	89	91	101	112	118	123	123	128	41	44	51	0	0	0
South East	136	130	130	306	296	290	106	110	114	193	202	200	121	121	134	172	183	178	196	184	181
South West	120	121	121	291	298	293	102	105	119	127	120	113	88	88	101	96	106	119	62	65	56
Wales	114	117	117	262	231	228	96	97	114	83	87	95	77	77	72	33	49	33	19	19	16
West Midlands	104	103	103	268	276	263	153	165	156	132	121	122	71	71	72	61	81	86	95	99	105
Yorkshire/Humber	105	103	103	273	266	255	82	83	89	98	104	104	71	71	66	36	38	39	81	89	78

Table 8.8: EU Regional Innovation Scoreboard 2006 UK data
Source: EU Trend Chart (2006)
Key: HRSTC – Knowledge workers, LIFE-LONG – Life-long learning, MED/HI-TEC – Med/Hi-tech manufacturing, HI-TECH – Hi-tech services, PUB R&D – Public R&D, BUS R&D – Business R&D, Patents.

The EU Regional Innovation Scoreboard 2006 UK composite indicator scores are shown in Table 8.9 for RNSII, REUSII and RRSII T-4, T-3, T-2, T-1 and T.

	RNSII					REUSII					RRSII				
	T-4	T-3	T-2	T-1	T	T-4	T-3	T-2	T-1	T	T-4	T-3	T-2	T-1	T
United Kingdom	0.55	0.52	0.52	0.48	0.49	0.65	0.68	0.66	0.64	0.63					
East Midlands	0.48	0.46	0.46	0.41	0.45	0.6	0.64	0.62	0.59	0.6	0.57	0.59	0.58	0.54	0.57
Eastern	0.69	0.66	0.67	0.58	0.59	0.75	0.78	0.77	0.73	0.72	0.73	0.75	0.74	0.7	0.69
London	0.53	0.53	0.52	0.46	0.48	0.64	0.69	0.66	0.63	0.63	0.61	0.65	0.63	0.59	0.59
North East	0.41	0.4	0.34	0.32	0.36	0.54	0.59	0.53	0.52	0.52	0.51	0.54	0.48	0.47	0.48
North West	0.5	0.46	0.43	0.41	0.42	0.62	0.64	0.6	0.6	0.58	0.59	0.59	0.56	0.55	0.54
Northern Ireland	0.23	0.22	0.26	0.24	0.27	0.43	0.47	0.49	0.47	0.46	0.38	0.41	0.44	0.41	0.41
Scotland	0.35	0.3	0.29	0.3	0.31	0.52	0.53	0.52	0.52	0.5	0.48	0.48	0.46	0.47	0.45
South East	0.75	0.7	0.71	0.65	0.63	0.78	0.81	0.79	0.78	0.75	0.77	0.78	0.77	0.75	0.72
South West	0.55	0.5	0.49	0.47	0.47	0.64	0.66	0.64	0.64	0.62	0.62	0.62	0.6	0.6	0.58
Wales	0.35	0.32	0.31	0.3	0.35	0.51	0.54	0.52	0.51	0.52	0.47	0.48	0.46	0.46	0.48
West Midlands	0.53	0.51	0.49	0.45	0.47	0.63	0.66	0.63	0.61	0.61	0.6	0.62	0.6	0.57	0.57
Yorkshire/Humber	0.39	0.37	0.36	0.35	0.37	0.53	0.56	0.55	0.54	0.53	0.5	0.52	0.5	0.49	0.49

Table 8.9: EU Regional Innovation Scoreboard 2006 UK composite indicator scores
Source: EU Trend Chart (2006)
Key: RNSII – Regional National Summary Innovation Index, REUSII – Regional European Summary Innovation Index, RRSII – Revealed Regional Summary Innovation index (RRSII).

The composite indicator scores in Table 8.9 take the average for RNSII, REUSII and RRSII T-4, T-3, T-2, T-1 and T (consistent with the findings Table 8.6).

Table 8.10 shows nine UK Regional Innovation Indicators for the 12 regions compared with those for the EU.

REGION	INDICATOR																	
	1		2		3		4		5		6		7		8		9	
European Union	21.78	a	8.52	a	7.41	a	3.57	a	0.68	b	1.3	b	31.6	b	161.1	b	22603	c
United Kingdom	29.36	a	22.29	a	6.72	a	4.47	a	0.6	d	1.28	b	35.6	b	133.5	b	26096	c
East Midlands	24.29	a	21.12	a	7.93	a	3.96	a	0.38	d	1.45	b	13.5	b	108.9	b	24411	c
Eastern	26.96	a	23.04	a	7.6	a	5.35	a	0.55	d	3.11	b	94.2	b	261.3	b	27031	c
London	41.66	a	25.2	a	2.45	a	6.23	a	0.64	d	0.41	b	41	b	112.5	b	38230	c
North East	22.41	a	20.43	a	8.82	a	3.14	a	0.38	d	0.35	b	6	b	64.6	b	20136	c
North West	24.8	a	21.22	a	7.22	a	3.59	a	0.34	d	1.52	b	12.2	b	103.4	b	22670	c
Northern Ireland	25.23	a	14.69	a	5.75	a	2.6	a	0.38	d	0.69	b	7.7	b	42.5	b	20224	c
Scotland	32.83	a	21.88	a	5.75	a	3.28	a	0.82	d	0.62	b	18	b	91.2	b	25290	c
South East	33.78	a	24.11	a	7.28	a	6.25	a	0.78	d	2.49	b	74.6	b	233.2	b	28754	c
South West	29.34	a	22.98	a	6.98	a	4.1	a	0.6	d	1.37	b	49.6	b	145.4	b	23675	c
Wales	26.13	a	19.94	a	6.58	a	2.69	a	0.49	d	0.34	b	10.4	b	69.9	b	20959	c
West Midlands	25.45	a	21.41	a	10.49	a	4.28	a	0.46	d	0.78	b	11.8	b	97.3	b	23919	c
Yorkshire/Humber	25.09	a	21.76	a	5.59	a	3.16	a	0.46	d	0.4	b	15.3	b	86.9	b	22927	c

Key: Year a 2002 b 2001 c 2000 d 1999

Indicator
1 Tertiary education
2 Lifelong learning
3 Med/hi-tech employment in manufacturing
4 High-tech employment in services
5 Public R&D
6 Business R&D
7 High-tech patent applications
8 Patent applications
9 GDP per capita

Table 8.10: UK Regional Innovation Indicators Source: EC (2003)

Using the initial framework for identifying indicators relevant to small firms (Table 8.5) for the three performance areas of generation of new knowledge (public R&D), industry-science linkages (med/high tech employment in manufacturing and high-tech patent applications) and industrial innovation (business R&D and patent applications) a comparison of regional profiles can be made.

Conclusions

The chapter has reviewed the current innovation performance indicators relevant to small firms and has presented an approach that can be used to provide analysis of innovation activity for the comparison of countries and regions. A framework for selecting and placing indicators in three performance areas has been explored. Results according to the performance areas have been derived from databases including the EC and OECD. The chapter identifies those indicators useful to entrepreneurs, policy makers, practitioners, researchers and educators and these include public R&D, med/high tech employment in manufacturing, high tech patent applications, business R&D and patent applications.

Recommended Reading

Thomas, B. and Murphy, L. (2009) A review of innovation performance indicators relevant to small firms in Wales, *32nd Institute for Small Business and Entrepreneurship Conference*, 3-6 November, ISBE Handbook, Liverpool.

References

Acs, Z.J. and Audretsch, D.B. (1990) *Innovation and Small Firms*, Cambridge Mass: MIT Press.

Acs, Z.J. and Audretsch, D.B. (1993) Analysing innovation output indicators: the US experience. In: Kleinknecht, A., Bain, D. (Eds.), *New Concepts in Innovation Output Measurement*, St. Martin's Press, New York, pp. 10–41.

Audretsch, D.B. and Feldman, M.P. (1996a) Innovative Clusters and the Industry Life-cycle, *The Review of Industrial Organization*, 11, pp. 253-273.

Audretsch, D.B. and Feldman, M.P. (1996b) Knowledge spillovers and the geography of innovation and production, *American Economic Review*, 86, pp. 630–640.

Audretsch, D.B. and Stephan, P.E. (1996) Company-scientist locational links: the case of biotechnology, *The American Economic Review*, 86(3), pp. 641–652.

Audretsch, D.B. (1995) Innovation, growth and survival, *International Journal of Industrial Organization*, 13(4), pp. 441-457.

Conference Board of Canada (CBC) (2004) Exploring Canada's Innovation Character: Benchmarking Against Global Best, CBC, Ottawa, Ontario, June.

Dunne, T. (1994) Plant age and technology use in U.S. manufacturing industries. *Rand Journal of Economics,* 25, pp. 488–499.

EU Trend Chart (2002) *European Trend Chart on Innovation*, http://trendchart.cordis.lu/scoreboards/Scoreboard2002/download_area.cfm (accessed 07/06/2007).

EU Trend Chart (2003) *European Trend Chart on Innovation*, http://trendchart.cordis.lu/scoreboards/scoreboard2003/scoreboard_papers.cfm (accessed 07/06/2007).

EU Trend Chart (2004) *Trend Chart Innovation Policy in Europe*, http://www.trendchart.org/scoreboards/scoreboard2004/indicators.cfm (accessed 07/06/2007).

EU Trend Chart (2006) *2006 European Regional Innovation Scoreboard* (2006 RIS), European Trend Chart on Innovation, MERIT – Maastricht Economic and social Research and training centre on Innovation and Technology), European Commission.

European Commission (EC) (2001) *European Innovation Scorebaord 2001*, Luxembourg, SEC 1414.

European Commission (EC), 2003; Third European Report on Science and Technology Indicators 2003, Brussels, EUR 20025 EN.

European Commission (EC) (2005) *European Innovation Scoreboard 2005*, Brussels.

European Innovation Scoreboard (EIS) (2009) *European Innovation Scoreboard 2008: Comparative Analysis of Innovation Performance*, January, http://www.proinno-europe.eu/metrics (accessed 03/08/2009).

Feldman, M., Link, A. and Siegel, D. (2002) *The Economics of Science and Technology*, Boston: Kluwer Academic Press.

Freudenberg, M. (2003) Composite indicators of country performance: A critical assessment, STI Working Paper 2003/16, Paris, OECD.

Grabowski, H.G. (1968) The Determinants of Industrial Research and Development: a study of the chemical, drug and petroleum industries, *Journal of Political Economy*, 72, pp. 292-306.

Griliches, Z. (1979) Issues in assessing the contribution of research and development to productivity growth, *The Bell Journal of Economics*, 10(1), pp. 92–116.

Grupp, H. and Mogee, M. (2004) Indicators for national science and technology policy: How robust are composite indicators, *Research Policy*, 33(9), pp. 1373-1384.
Grupp, H. (2006) How robust are composite innovation indicators for evaluating the performance of national innovation systems?, University of Karlsruhe and Fraunhofer ISI, Germany.

Hall, B., Griliches, Z. and Hausman, J. (1986) Patents and R&D: Is There a Lag? *International Economic Review*, 27(2), pp. 265-283.

Le Bail, F. (2006) *Innovating through EU Regional Policy*, DG Enterprise and Industry, European Commission, Brussels.

Link, A. and Rees, J. (1990) Firm size, university based research and the return on R&D, *Small Business Economics*, 2(1), pp. 25-32.

Mansfield, E. (1968) *The Economics of Technological Change*, New York: Norton.

Mueller, D. (1967) The Firm's Decision Process: An Econometric Investigation, *Quarterly Journal of Economics*, 32, pp. 58-87.

Nardo, M., Saisana, M., Saltelli, A. and Tarantola, S. (2005a) *Tools for Composite Indicators Building*, EC Joint Research Centre, EUR 21682.

Nardo, M., Saisana, M., Saltelli, A., Tarantola, S., Hoffman, A. and Giovannini, E. (2005b) *Handbook on constructing composite indicators: Methodology and user guide*, STI Statistics Working Paper, Paris, OECD.

National Endowment for Science, Technology and the Arts (NESTA) (2009) *Innovation Index Project, Private Sector Update*, May, http://www.innovationindex.org.uk (accessed 03/08/2009).

Organisation for Economic Co-operation and Development (OECD) (1997) The Measurement of Scientific and Technical Activities: Proposed Standard Practice for Surveys of Research and Experimental Development, Frascati Manual, OECD, Paris.

Organisation for Economic Co-operation and Development (OECD) (2001) *The New Economy: Beyond the Hype – The OECD Growth Project.*

Organisation for Economic Co-operation and Development (OECD) (2007) OECD *Glossary of Statistical Terms – NUTS classification,* http://stats.oecd.org/glossary/detail.asp?ID=6640 (accessed 07/06/2007).

Pakes, A. and Griliches, Z. (1980) Patents and R&D at the Firm Level: A First Look, *Economic Letters*, 5, pp. 377-381.

Prevezer, M. (1997) The dynamics of industrial clustering in biotechnology, *Small Business Economics*, 9, pp. 255–271.

Romeo, A.A. (1975) Interindustry and interfirm differences in the rate of diffusion of an innovation, *The Review of Economics and Statistics*, 57, pp. 311–319.

Saisana, M. and Tarantola, S. (2002) State-of-the-art Report on Current Methodologies and Practices for Composite Indicator Development, EC Joint Research Centre, EUR 20 408.

Scherer, F.M. (1965) Firm size, market structure, opportunity, and the output of patented inventions, *The American Economic Review*, 55, pp. 1097-1125.

Scherer, F.M. (1983) The propensity to patent, *International Journal of Industrial Organization*, 1(1), pp. 107-128.

Schubert, T. (2006) *How Robust are Rankings of Composite Indicators when Weights are Changed, Proposing a New Methodology*, Trest Conference "Neo-Schumpeterian Economics: An Agenda for the 21st Century".

Schumpeter, J. (1934) *The Theory of Economic Development*, Oxford: Oxford University Press.

Schwalbach, J. and Zimmermann, K.F. (1991) A Poisson Model of Patenting and Firm Structure in Germany, in Acs, Z.J. and Audretsch, D.B. (Eds.) *Innovation and Technological Change: An International Comparison*, Ann Arbor: University of Michigan Press, pp. 109-120.

Sharpe, A. and Guilbaud, O. (2005) *Indicators of Innovation in Canadian Natural Resource Industries*, Centre for the Study of Living Standards for Natural Resources Canada, CSLS Research Report, Ontario.

Siegel, D.S. (1999) *Skill-Based Technological Change: Evidence From a Firm-Level Study*, W.E. Upjohn Institute for Employment Research.

Stead, H. (2001) *The Development of S&T Statistics in Canada: An Informal Account*, Paper No. 5, Project on the History and Sociology of S&T Statistics.

Veugelers, R. (2005) *Assessing Innovation Capacity: Fitting Strategy, Indicators and Policy to the Right Framework*, paper presented to Advancing Knowledge and the Knowledge Economy, National Academy of Sciences, Washington, D.C.

9. Conclusions

"Creativity is thinking up new things. Innovation is doing new things."
                                                    THEODORE LEVITT (1925-2006)

Introduction
It is possible to relate the body of knowledge encompassed within technological innovation theory to an understanding of the processes involved in small business innovation support networks through the dichotomy of near and supra-national technology transfer networks. Near technology transfer networks operate at regional level and involve industrial clusters with overarching innovation policies guided by local and regional government bodies.

Invention, Innovation and Small Business
The question that arises is whether policy makers should leave inventors alone and let market forces take effect or should they intervene? On previous evidence (Gornall and Thomas, 2001) it appears that they should intervene due to the specific requirements of many individual inventors involved with small businesses and the need to provide them with support (Meyer, 2005). This is a problem that appears to be the case in most economies. The harnessing of peripheral individual talent through a 'coupling' process can yield unrealised benefits to the economic development of regions and countries. Moreover, strategies will need to be formulated to release and realise the significant benefits of this indigenous talent but it is evident that larger studies should be undertaken in order to shape future political strategies of our knowledge economies.

Research and Development and the Small Firm
It has been recognised that the technological development of small businesses is influenced by various sources of know-how including R&D, industry contacts, learning, ICT and publications. R&D is therefore a major source for technological progress in the modern economy. A principal justification for support of R&D policy activities will rest upon the positive spillovers which are the positive externalities from R&D (Revesz and Boldeman, 2006). Studies undertaken in the literature have revealed the major concepts involved in the study of R&D in industrial sectors. In particular the importance of R&D in enhancing technology absorption is considered important for small businesses.

Technology Diffusion

Although the variables involved in models applicable to technology diffusion into small businesses appear to be the most important influences on diffusion there will also be a multiplicity of influences that accelerate or alleviate the rate of diffusion. This spectrum of influences on diffusion rates broadens when considering technology transfer among various different small businesses in multi-tiered networks. In these small firms' sociological forces have an important role to play. Rate of adoption of a new technology will be faster if it is compatible with previous experience and present normative values of small businesses. Other influences on speed of diffusion include complexity of new technology and random influences involved with clusters and networks.

Clusters and Knowledge Flows

Within a cluster a number of mechanisms for the transfer of knowledge have been identified by Keeble and Wilkinson (1999) and these include new firms, spin-offs from firms, universities and public sector research laboratories, interactions between the makers and users of capital equipment, interactions between customers and suppliers, and inter-firm mobility of the labour in the cluster. Relationships and mechanisms create flows within the cluster and the knowledge transfer processes result in cumulative know-how that is external to firms remaining internal to the cluster (Oliver and Porta, 2006). Empirical evidence has shown how knowledge sustainability (expenditure on education), regional economic outputs (earnings and labour productivity), knowledge capital (patents and R&D) and human capital (high tech employment) have influenced regional competitiveness (Porter, 1990). Economic productive activities are enabled by tacit knowledge, the contribution of local small businesses and infrastructures such as research institutes and universities, by employee exchange and the mobilisation of human capital resources (Oliver and Porta, 2006).

Higher Education Spin-offs

Spin-off enterprises are companies whose activities are based on technologies developed as a result of academic research programmes. Such companies are significant in a local economic development context, in that they are likely to lead to the commercialisation of research in fairly close proximity to the Higher Education Institution (HEI) involved. This has benefit for both the local economy and the HEI itself. Risks and problems in forming and growing spin-off companies must not be underestimated, and it is important to recognise that they represent a significant route to the commercial exploitation of new ideas and technologies. In appropriate circumstances they can make an important contribution to regional and national prosperity. A critical challenge for HEIs is to ensure that where a spin-off is an appropriate vehicle, it is properly managed and there are structures to enable its true potential to be realised.

Global Start-ups

A form of Higher Education spin-off is a global start-up which has developed from an academic institution. Here it is particularly interesting that in the discussion on international, cross-cultural and comparative academic research about entrepreneurs, including corporate "intrapreneurs" and founders of domestic new ventures, it appears that global start-ups play a significant role. An important aspect of this is the regional infrastructure for Higher Education global start-ups. Politics can change the regional potential to support global start-ups, both in terms of how the system is organised and how clients experience the system if appropriate support is provided to these types of companies which need to take into account indicators of their innovation performance.

Innovation Performance Indicators

Through the development of innovation performance indicators it is possible to develop more advanced and accurate measures of innovation activity for small businesses to ensure better benchmarking of progress for economies. Although innovation performance indicators have many methodological shortcomings the construction of consistent and comparable indicators are important for the analysis of small businesses policy in countries. Through following a methodology that is recognised at an international level it is believed that this will lead to robust results. This is an appropriate response to the current knowledge gap regarding the measurement of innovative activity, since it is possible to investigate the difficult issues surrounding the identification and accurate measurement of data on innovation.

www.ingramcontent.com/pod-product-compliance
Lightning Source LLC
Chambersburg PA
CBHW081416080526
44589CB00016B/2557